...n guide in the *Concentrate* series shows you what to ...ect in your law exam, what examiners are looking for, ...how to achieve extra marks.

Written by experts
Developed with students
Designed for success

For a full lis... ...s available and ...oming please visit th... ...site

Visit **www.oxfordtextbooks.co.uk/orc/concentrate/** for a wealth of online resources including a podcast of exam and revision guidance, diagnostic tests, understanding your marks, interactive flashcard glossaries and cases, and multiple-choice questions

Acknowledgements

I owe a debt of gratitude to the Law School at the University of West London, which is committed to a practical and interactive approach to law teaching as well as the implementation of online learning. I wish to acknowledge the kindness of Ms Nina Scott who initially gave me the opportunity to teach Public Law in 1989 and encouraged me in my early years of teaching and the help and support of Ms Scott's successor the late Mr William Brown. I also wish to acknowledge the contributions made by Toufik Meddah LL.B Hons, a former student, to the development of the pedagogic features and current debates sections, and to the research and writing of the new chapter on tribunals. Finally, I wish to thank all my colleagues at the University of West London, past and present, without whose kindness, help, and support this book could never have been contemplated, let alone written.

The figure in chapter 9 is reproduced from the Senior President of Tribunals' Annual Report (February 2011) under the Open Government Licence.

QR Codes are used throughout this book. QR Code is a registered trademark of DENSO WAVE INCORPORATED. You can scan the code with your mobile device to launch the relevant webpage from the Online Resource Centre. If your mobile device does not have a QR Code reader try this website for advice www.mobile-barcodes.com/qr-code-software.

New to this edition

An entirely new chapter on tribunals.
Up to date information on the Tribunals, Courts and Enforcement Act 2007.
Up to date information on the Constitutional Reform and Governance Act 2010.
Up to date information on the Parliamentary Voting and Constituencies Act 2011.
New cases on the royal prerogative, separation of powers, police powers, terrorism, and judicial review.
Heavily revised chapters on judicial review and the executive.

Public Law
Concentrate

2nd edition

Colin Faragher

Senior Lecturer in Law
University of West London

OXFORD
UNIVERSITY PRESS

OXFORD
UNIVERSITY PRESS

Great Clarendon Street, Oxford OX2 6DP

Oxford University Press is a department of the University of Oxford.
It furthers the University's objective of excellence in research, scholarship,
and education by publishing worldwide in

Oxford New York

Auckland Cape Town Dar es Salaam Hong Kong Karachi
Kuala Lumpur Madrid Melbourne Mexico City Nairobi
New Delhi Shanghai Taipei Toronto

With offices in

Argentina Austria Brazil Chile Czech Republic France Greece
Guatemala Hungary Italy Japan Poland Portugal Singapore
South Korea Switzerland Thailand Turkey Ukraine Vietnam

Oxford is a registered trade mark of Oxford University Press
in the UK and in certain other countries

Published in the United States
by Oxford University Press Inc., New York

British Library Cataloguing in Publication Data
Data available

Library of Congress Cataloging in Publication Data
Data available

Typeset by Newgen Imaging Systems (P) Ltd, Chennai, India
Printed in Great Britain
on acid-free paper by
Ashford Colour Press Ltd, Gosport, Hampshire

ISBN 978–0–19–960948–2

10 9 8 7 6 5 4 3 2 1

Contents

Table of cases

Table of cases

****

Table of cases
✳✳✳✳✳✳✳✳✳✳

Table of legislation

Statutes

Table of legislation

Table of legislation

****

#1

Introduction to constitutional law

Key Facts

- A constitution is a document or set of documents intentionally drafted to form the fundamental law of a country.

- Constitutional law in the United Kingdom comes from statutes, the common law, and political rules called constitutional conventions.

- Constitutions may be classified as written or unwritten, flexible or rigid, monarchical or republican, federal or unitary, supreme or subordinate to the legislature, or based on the separation of powers.

- The British Constitution is unwritten, flexible, monarchical, unitary, subordinate to the legislature, and based on a partial or a limited degree of separation of powers.

- The constitutional framework of the United Kingdom is provided by statutes.

****

What is constitutional law?

'Constitutional law' has a variety of meanings.

Constitutional law is a body of legal rules and political arrangements concerning the government of a country. A constitution is a document or set of documents which may declare that a country legitimately exists following a revolution or independence from colonial rule. It may declare, among other things, the legal name of the country and describe its national symbols like the flag and the national anthem. It may also identify the national language. Most constitutions describe the purpose, powers, structure, and personnel of a country's organs of government as well as fundamental human rights.

The classification of constitutions

KC Wheare in *Modern Constitutions*, 2nd edn (1966) identifies six ways of classifying constitutions.

Written and unwritten

Countries with a document or set of documents intentionally drafted to be the fundamental law of the country have a written constitution. 'Fundamental' means that this document or set of documents may require a special procedure to create and amend it. All organs of government, including the legislature, must act in a way which is compatible with it. The courts have jurisdiction to interpret and enforce the constitution. This may or may not be done by a special constitutional court. Countries which do not have such a document or set of documents have an unwritten constitution.

Flexible and rigid

Where no special process is required to amend a constitution it is called 'flexible'. Where a special process is required a constitution is called 'rigid'.

Supreme or subordinate to the legislature

Chief Justice Marshall in the US Supreme Court decision in *Marbury v Madison* (1803) said that an act of the legislature which is repugnant to the constitution is void. This means that the constitution is supreme and that the legislature must act in a way which is consistent with the constitution.

In countries with an unwritten constitution the legislature is supreme. It can make or unmake any law it likes and the courts have no jurisdiction to question the validity of a statute.

Federal or unitary constitutions

In a federal constitution the governmental powers are divided between a central government, which may be called the Federal Government, and state, regional, or provincial governments. Each state, region, or province has its own government. Moreover, each state, region or province, while being a member of the federation, is independent in its own sphere. The central or federal government exercises the constitutional powers expressly granted to it by the states, regions or provinces. It does so independently within its own sphere.

In a unitary state all governmental powers originate from the central or national government. The central or national government can transfer powers to regional and local authorities but these remain subordinate to the central or national government and can be overridden by it.

Constitutions based or not based on the separation of powers

It is very difficult, if not impossible, to find a state where there is a complete separation of powers. In such a hypothetical system the legislature, executive, and judiciary should check and balance each other as they each exercise their powers independently. No one person should be able to exercise power over all the organs and functions of government.

Republican and monarchical constitutions

Where the head of state is a president a country may be called a **republic**. If a country has a hereditary head of state it may be called a monarchy.

Revision tip

Go online and look up a selection of constitutions, which illustrate the classification of constitutions. Think about how each constitution fits into the appropriate classification.

The sources of constitutional law

The sources of constitutional law in the United Kingdom are statutes and the **common law**.

In *Thoburn v Sunderland City Council* (2003) Laws LJ said that the law should recognise a hierarchy of Acts of Parliament based on the distinction between 'ordinary' and 'constitutional' statutes. He went on to say that a constitutional statute:

(a) conditions the legal relationship between the citizen and state in some general, overarching manner; or

(b) enlarges or diminishes the scope of fundamental constitutional rights.

The sources of constitutional law
****

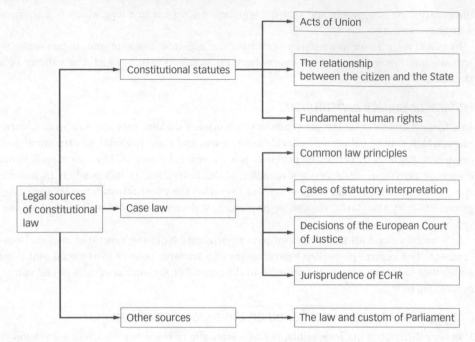

Figure 1.1

Laws LJ concluded that the special status of constitutional statutes follows the special status of constitutional rights. He went on to say that constitutional statutes included **Magna Carta 1297**, the **Bill of Rights 1689**, the **Union with Scotland Act 1706**, the **Reform Acts** which distributed and enlarged the franchise (**Representation of the People Acts 1832, 1867, and 1884**), **the Human Rights Act 1998**, the **Scotland Act 1998**, and the **Government of Wales Act 1998**. Finally, he said that the **European Communities Act 1972** is also a constitutional statute because it incorporated into UK law the whole body of substantive Community rights and obligations, and gave overriding domestic effect to the judicial and administrative machinery of Community law.

Revision tip

When discussing sources of constitutional law in an essay question it is important to compare, contrast, and critically evaluate the traditional view and the new perspective concerning constitutional statutes.

✔ Looking for extra marks?

The issues discussed in this chapter can give rise to some very elaborate arguments. You should follow up the issues raised here in your recommended standard textbook. You should also read the articles recommended below.

 **Key cases**

Case	Facts	Principle
International Transport Roth GmbH v Secretary of State for the Home Department [2003] QB 728	This concerned the relationship between EU and UK law.	The British system stands at an intermediate stage between parliamentary supremacy and constitutional supremacy. The common law recognizes and endorses the notion of fundamental or constitutional rights.
R v Secretary of State for Transport, ex p Factortame (No 1) [1990] 2 AC 85	This was an application for judicial review of the provisions of the Merchant Shipping Act 1988.	In so far as the applicants succeed before the ECJ in obtaining a ruling in support of the Community rights which they claim, those rights will prevail over the restrictions imposed on registration of British fish ing vessels by Pt II of the Act of 1988 and the Divisional Court will, in the final determination of the application for judicial review, be obliged to make appropriate declarations to give effect to those rights.
R (on the application of Jackson) v Attorney General [2006] 1 AC 262	This concerned the validity of the Parliament Act 1949.	There is no constitutional principle or principle of statutory interpretation which prohibits the UK Parliament from altering its own constitution by enacting alterations to the statute from which these powers come provided the power extends that far.
R (on the application of Southall) v Secretary of State for Foreign and Commonwealth Affairs [2003] 3 CMLR 18	This was an application for declarations that ratification of draft Treaty establishing a constitution for Europe would be unlawful and/or contrary to convention without prior electoral approval.	No court has jurisdiction to set aside any provision of an Act of Parliament on the basis that it is unlawful, save in circumstances set out in the European Communities Act 1972. A court cannot determine that an Act of Parliament passed without first having been the subject of a referendum or being included in a party manifesto is unenforceable as a matter of law.
Thoburn v Sunderland City Council [2003] QB 151	This concerned weights and measures legislation and EU law.	There are now two categories of statute within the UK: 1. constitutional statutes; 2. ordinary statutes. Ordinary statutes are subject to implied repeal. Constitutional Statutes are not.

Key debates

****

 Key debates

Topic	**'What is a Political Constitution?'**
Name	Graham Gee
Viewpoint	Analyses the notion of a 'political constitution' as it purports to describe the constitution in a jurisdiction, such as the UK, which lacks a legal constitution. Compares the accounts of the UK Constitution by JAG Griffith, Adam Tomkins, and Richard Bellamy.
Source	(2010) Oxford Journal of Legal Studies 30(2), 273–299

Topic	**'Constitutional Statutes'**
Name	Editorial
Viewpoint	Comments on the identification in the Administrative Court judgment in *Thoburn v Sunderland City Council* (2003) of a distinction between 'ordinary' and 'constitutional' statutes, the latter being characterized by their treatment of overarching issues of citizens' fundamental rights, and by the fact that they cannot be repealed by implication. Considers some examples of supposed constitutional statutes to determine whether the classification offers any real legal value.
Source	(2007) Statute Law Review 28(2), iii-v

Topic	**'Defending deference in public law and constitutional theory'**
Name	Aileen Kavanagh
Viewpoint	Explores the idea of judicial deference to legislative and governmental decisions which is currently a very controversial area of public law in the United Kingdom.
Source	**(2010)** Law Quarterly Review 222.

Topic	**'Constitutional Issues and Structures'**
Name	John Alder
Viewpoint	Political and legal aspects of a constitution, although overlapping, should be distinguished. There is a tendency in any form of government for powers to gravitate towards a single group so that a primary concern of constitutional law is to provide checks and balances between different branches of government. The Constitution of the UK is parliamentary, unitary, unwritten, and heavily reliant on non-legal mechanisms.
	The distinction between written and unwritten constitutions is of some but not fundamental importance. The UK Constitution is an untidy mixture of different kinds of law practices and customs and has a substantial informal element, lending itself to domination by personal networks. It is questionable whether the UK Constitution can be rationalized in terms of consistent general principles. However, at the other extreme, it might be more than just what happens.
Source	*Constitutional and Administrative Law*, 8th edn (2011).

Topic	'Classification of Constitutions'
Name	Neil Walker
Viewpoint	Argues that unitary conception of constitution is very flexible. Fundamental limits set by unitary conception are not great. Competition between state and other authorities militates against transformation of unitary conception.
Source	[2000] PL 384.

 Exam question

Essay question

Explain what is meant by 'Constitution' and how constitutions might be classified.

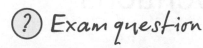 Scan here

Scan this QR code image with your mobile device to see an outline answer to this question or log onto www.oxfordtextbooks.co.uk/orc/concentrate

#2

Sources of constitutional law: constitutional conventions

Key Facts

- British constitutional law is founded upon statutory and common law rules.

- These play an important role in the process of government.

- Vitally important parts of the process of government in the UK are regulated by binding political rules and practices called 'constitutional conventions'.

- There is an identifiable distinction between binding constitutional conventions and non-binding 'practices'.

- Some writers suggest that they can be recognized and stated with precision by applying the appropriate test.

- The courts have no jurisdiction to grant a remedy where the sole basis of the claim is that a constitutional convention has been breached.

- The only way a constitutional convention can become law is by statute.

What are constitutional conventions?

What are constitutional conventions?

Revision tip

Essay questions on this topic are common. Make sure you understand the arguments dealing with the basis and validity of the distinction between laws and conventions.

AV Dicey, in *Introduction to the Study of the Law of the Constitution* (1885), distinguished between laws and conventions. Laws are enforceable in the courts. Conventions are not: there are no judicial remedies or penalties if conventions are violated.

Enforceability and the distinction between laws and conventions

Although Sir Ivor Jennings, in *Cabinet Government* (1969), said that constitutional conventions are outside the law and not recognized by it, he used cases like *Watt v Kesteven County Council* (1955) to claim that not all legal provisions confer directly enforceable rights on the individual. The Court of Appeal had to decide whether a local education authority was in breach of statutory duty because it had failed to provide education for pupils in accordance with the wishes of their parents as required by **s 76** of the **Education Act 1944**. Denning LJ held that the duty to make schools available could be enforced only by the minister and that **s 76** did not create a cause of action entitling an individual to a remedy in the civil courts.

Munro's response to this is that the court refused to recognise an actionable statutory duty because the law said that the duty should not be enforced in this way. The law was enforced. The courts obeyed the law and put it into effect.

Revision tip

Views expressed in the standard textbooks are important in constitutional law. In essay questions on this topic you should be able to compare and contrast the arguments advanced by leading authorities. This will make your answer stand out.

Are laws and conventions different in kind?

In *Cabinet Government* (1969) Sir Ivor Jennings said that laws and conventions work in similar ways and that both are obeyed by those to whom they apply. Some conventions were as fixed as laws and could be stated with as much precision. JDB Mitchell, in *Constitutional Law*, 2nd edn (1968) said that it may be wrong to distinguish between laws and conventions because both were based on precedent and can overlap. Munro, in *Studies in Constitutional Law* (1999), says that nothing in Mitchell's argument demonstrates conclusively that distinguishing between laws and conventions will fail. Munro concludes that conventions and laws appear to be similar because they are both rules operating in society. They are not necessarily the same because they look similar.

Are there different categories of constitutional conventions?

Dicey focuses on the purpose of law and the jurisdiction of the courts. He was aware that there are different classes of rules. Some conventions are as important as laws. As political rules they are obeyed to a greater or lesser degree. Maitland, in *The Constitutional History of England* (1961), also recognized that such rules differed in stringency and definiteness. Munro, in *Studies in Constitutional Law* (1999), agreed with Maitland. Munro concluded that it was sensible to have a two-class approach where it is clear that groups of uniform non-legal rules of a high degree of stringency and definiteness exist. Where such uniformity does not exist a two-class approach is not so easily achieved.

Are all constitutional conventions binding?

Constitutional conventions are, generally speaking, binding political rules. Some authorities, however, distinguish between binding and non-binding political rules. For instance KC Wheare, in *The Statute of Westminister and Dominion Status*, 5th edn (1953) said that there were usages and conventions. According to Wheare, a constitutional convention is binding. A usage is a non-binding rule of political practice. A usage may become a convention from a single precedent or by agreement. Many authorities have adopted a similar approach. Hood Phillips and Jackson, in *Constitutional and Administrative Law* (2001), for instance, incorporate the distinction between usages and conventions into their definition of constitutional conventions. JDB Mitchell, in *Constitutional Law*, 2nd edn (1968), also stressed the need to distinguish between non-binding political practices and binding constitutional conventions. De Smith and Brazier, in *Constitutional and Administrative Law* (1998), said that conventions were forms of political behaviour regarded as binding, and as such were distinguishable from non-binding usage. G Marshall and GC Moodie in *Some Problems of the Constitution* (1971) draw a distinction between obligatory and non-obligatory rules. A rule must prescribe something if it is to guide action or state obligations. The true basis for a rule is prescription not description: description is not a weak form of prescription.

Revision tip

To obtain top marks you must be aware of current debates and critical thinking.

Examples of constitutional conventions

Royal Assent

Legal rules

Every bill which has passed the necessary parliamentary stages must receive the **Royal Assent** in order to become an Act of Parliament. **The Parliament Acts 1911** and **1949** permit a bill to become an Act without assent of the House of Lords. Certain procedures surrounding the Royal Assent are governed by the **Royal Assent Act 1967**. The reigning monarch is not legally bound to grant the Royal Assent.

Constitutional conventions

The monarch will grant the Royal Assent to a bill which has either been passed by the House of Commons and the House of Lords or has received the assent of the House of Commons under the **Parliament Acts 1911 and 1949**.

Appointment of the Prime Minister

Legal rules

At common law, under the **Royal Prerogative**, the Monarch has unlimited power to appoint ministers, including the Prime Minister.

Constitutional conventions

The Government must have the confidence of a majority in the House of Commons. This means that the Prime Minister is appointed from the membership of the House of Commons. The Prime Minister is normally the leader of the political party with a majority of seats in the House of Commons. If the party of which the Prime Minister is a member, loses its majority in the House of Commons, he, and the other members of the Government, will normally resign before the first meeting of the new Parliament.

Constitutional conventions and 'hung parliaments'

A hung parliament arises when, following a General Election, no party has an overall majority in the House of Commons.

In 'The 2010 General Election Outcome and the Formation of the Conservative – Liberal Democrat Coalition Government' (2011) Public Law 30–55 Robert Blackburn identifies three constitutional conventions which apply to hung parliaments. The first is that the incumbent Prime Minister has the first opportunity to continue in office and form an administration. The second is that if he is unable to do so (and resigns, or is defeated on the Address or in a no confidence motion at the meeting of the new Parliament) then the Leader of the Opposition is appointed Prime Minister. Thirdly, it is for the political parties to negotiate any inter-party agreement for government among themselves without royal involvement.

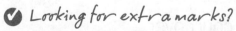 **Looking for extra marks?**

Robert Blackburn's article gives a valuable insight into how the constitutional conventions concerning hung parliaments are determined, interpreted, and applied in the factual context of the formation of the Conservative Liberal Democrat Coalition Government. It also shows how new conventions might be developed. You should read his article.

The appointment of ministers

Legal rules

There are no legal rules governing the appointment of ministers beyond the Royal Prerogative at common law and those contained in the **House of Commons (Disqualification) Act 1975,** which limits the number of ministers that may be appointed from the membership of the House of Commons to 95. Once they are appointed, statutes like the **Parliamentary and Other Pensions Act 1972** and the **Ministerial and Other Pensions and Salaries Act 1991** govern the payment of salaries and pensions.

Constitutional conventions

The constitutional conventions which govern the appointment of ministers are, firstly, that the monarch appoints ministers upon the advice of the Prime Minister and secondly that ministers are individually responsible to parliament.

This means that ministers are appointed from the membership of the House of Commons and the House of Lords.

The Cabinet

Legal rules

The Cabinet is recognized in statutes concerning ministerial salaries and pensions.

Constitutional conventions

The most important constitutional convention governing the Cabinet is collective Cabinet responsibility. This means that members of the Cabinet do not voice dissent on government policy once a decision is taken. A Cabinet minister who cannot sustain a Cabinet decision should resign.

✅ *Looking for extra marks?*

The constitutional conventions discussed above are a selection. To gain a fuller knowledge of the true extent and significance of constitutional conventions you should read your recommended standard textbook.

Revision tip

After being able to define constitutional conventions and explain how they are different from laws, you should be prepared to identify the elements of the most important constitutional conventions.

What is the jurisdiction of the court over constitutional conventions?

Dicey's answer is that constitutional conventions are not legal rules because the courts have no power (jurisdiction) to enforce them.

Madzimbamuto v Lardner-Burke [1969] 1 AC 645

After the unlawful declaration of independence by the Government of the Crown Colony of Southern Rhodesia in 1965, the United Kingdom Parliament passed the **Southern Rhodesia Act 1965** to deal with the circumstances arising from this unconstitutional action. In this case, the question was whether or not Parliament could properly legislate for Southern Rhodesia.

The relevant constitutional convention was that the Parliament at Westminster would not legislate for Southern Rhodesia on matters within the competence of the Legislative Assembly of Southern Rhodesia except with the agreement of the Southern Rhodesia Government.

The key principle is that a constitutional convention has no legal effect in limiting the legislative power of Parliament.

The Privy Council held, by majority, that Parliament could properly legislate for Southern Rhodesia.

In *Attorney General v Jonathan Cape Ltd* (1975) the Attorney General sought permanent **injunctions** restraining the publishers Jonathan Cape Ltd as well as a newspaper from publishing the diaries or extracts from the diaries of former Cabinet Minister Richard Crossman. The diaries contained accounts of disagreements on matters of policy and details of discussions concerning the appointment of senior civil servants.

The Attorney General argued that all cabinet papers, discussions, and proceedings were confidential and the court should restrain any disclosure if the public interest in concealment outweighed the public interest in the right to free publication.

The relevant constitutional convention was joint Cabinet responsibility: any policy decision reached by the Cabinet has to be supported thereafter by all members of the Cabinet whether they approved of it or not, unless they feel compelled to resign.

The key principle is that the courts have jurisdiction to restrain publication of Cabinet material provided it can be shown, firstly that such publication will be a breach of confidence and, secondly, that there is no other facet of the public interest in conflict with and more compelling than that relied upon.

The judge decided to refuse to grant the injunctions. The contents of the first volume of the Crossman Diaries were such that their publication, after the lapse of nearly ten years, could not inhibit free discussion in the existing Cabinet and would not, therefore, prejudice the maintenance of the doctrine of joint cabinet responsibility.

Can the courts do anything with a constitutional convention?

Although the courts do not grant remedies for breach of constitutional conventions, they do sometimes look at them, at least indirectly, in the course of legal proceedings. There are two principles. The first is that the courts may be prepared to take constitutional conventions into account and give an opinion as to their existence and extent and, secondly, that the courts can take constitutional conventions into account to interpret the statutes or commonwealth constitutions.

Examples of constitutional conventions

****

The first principle is supported by *Liversidge v Anderson* **(1942)**. **Regulation 18B** of the **Defence (General) Regulations 1939** gave the Secretary of State for the Home Department the power to make orders to detain people if he had reasonable cause to believe that they were of hostile association. One such person brought an action against the Secretary of State for false imprisonment, which failed. In coming to its decision, the majority in the House of Lords took notice of the convention that the Secretary of State is answerable to Parliament under the doctrine of ministerial responsibility.

Sir Ivor Jennings, in *Cabinet Government* (1969), said that the existence of a constitutional convention can be determined by asking what are the precedents, do the actors in the precedents believe that they are bound by a rule, and is there a reason for the rule?

This test was accepted and applied by the Supreme Court of Canada in *Reference re Amendment to the Constitution of Canada* (1982). The court had to decide whether the Canadian Federal Government was bound by a constitutional convention to the effect that the Canadian Federal Parliament will not request an amendment to the constitutional statutes of Canada directly affecting federal/provincial relationships without prior consultation and agreement with the provinces. After applying Jennings' three questions above, a majority of the Supreme Court concluded that the alleged constitutional convention existed and that it would be unconstitutional for the proposals to go forward. The court did not enforce the convention. This was beyond the constitutional role of the judges.

In *R (on the application of Southall) v Secretary of State for Foreign & Commonwealth Affairs* (2003) the Court of Appeal had to decide whether there was a constitutional convention that a substantial constitutional change cannot be made (and therefore cannot be adopted) unless such a proposal has been approved by the electorate either as a result of the proposal being included in the manifesto of the party returned to government or in a referendum. The Court of Appeal was prepared to consider whether there was sufficient evidence that there was a convention that no Act of Parliament could be passed which altered UK constitutional law in a fundamental way without prior electoral approval. It was held that sufficient evidence was lacking and that even if there was a strong political case for a referendum this was not a matter for the courts.

The second principle is supported by the Privy Council decision in *Ibralebbe v R* **(1964)**. This case arose out of certain criminal appeals from Ceylon (now Sri Lanka). Basnayake CJ, in the Court of Criminal Appeal of Ceylon, held that, in effect, when Ceylon ceased to be a colony and became an independent sovereign state within the Commonwealth, the right of the Crown to hear criminal appeals ceased. The Judicial Committee of the Privy Council took jurisdiction and in so doing took into account the constitutional convention that the Order in Council accepting the Report of the Privy Council turns its report into the equivalent of a judgment of a court.

Revision tip

When answering examination questions, the most important thing is the general legal principle which forms the basis of the decision in each case. Essay questions may ask you to explore contextual issues or the significance of the rule.

Can constitutional conventions become law?

A constitutional convention can become law by statute. In 2006 the Joint Committee on Conventions was set up to consider the practicality of codifying the key conventions on the relationship between the two Houses of Parliament which affect the consideration of legislation. An example of how a convention might become law by statute is the codification of the Ponsonby Rule by the **Constitutional Reform and Governance Act 2010**. The Ponsonby Rule was a constitutional convention that treaties which did not come into force on signature, but which instead came into force later when governments expressed their consent to be bound through a formal act such as ratification, had to be laid before both Houses of Parliament as a Command Paper for a minimum period of 21 sitting days subject to a resolution of either House that it should not be ratified. The rule gave no legal effect to such a resolution. **Section 20(1)** of the **Constitutional Reform and Governance Act 2010** provides that a treaty cannot be ratified unless a minister of the Crown has laid a published copy it before Parliament which has 21 sitting days to object to its ratification by resolution.

Conventions cannot become part of the common law in the same way that customs are capable of doing. This was determined by the Court of Appeal in *Manuel v Attorney General* *(1982)*. This was an attempt to question the legality of the **Canada Act 1982** in the British courts by a minority group within Canada. It was suggested that the convention that the United Kingdom Parliament should not legislate for Canada except with its consent, might by formal recognition or by long acceptance have crystallized into a law. Slade LJ, giving the judgment of the Court, rejected this argument saying that it was 'quite unsustainable in the courts of this country'.

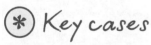 **Key cases**

Case	Facts	Principle
***Attorney General v Jonathan Cape Ltd* [1975] 3 All ER 484**	The Attorney General sought injunctions to restrain the publication of the diaries of a former Cabinet Minister.	A court can restrain publication of Cabinet material only where there is breach of confidence or that it is in the public interest to do so to protect collective Cabinet responsibility. But this lapses with time according to the circumstances of each case. Applying this principle, sufficient time had lapsed to allow publication.

Key cases

****

Case	Facts	Principle
Madzimbamuto v Lardner Burke [1969] 1 AC 645	The Privy Council had to decide whether the UK Parliament could legislate for Southern Rhodesia, following the Unilateral Declaration of Independence.	A constitutional convention, however important, can have no legal effect to limit the legislative supremacy of Parliament.
Manuel v Attorney General [1982] 3 All ER 822	This was an attempt to question the legality of the Canada Act 1982 in the British courts by a minority group within Canada. It was suggested that the convention that the United Kingdom Parliament should not legislate for Canada except with its consent, might by formal recognition or by long acceptance have crystallized into a law.	Conventions cannot become part of the Common Law in the same way that customs are capable of doing.
R (on the Application of Southall) v Secretary of State for Foreign and Commonwealth Affairs [2003] CMLR 18	This was an Appeal from the Administrative Court which had refused permission to proceed with Judicial Review. One of the issues was whether it is a convention of the constitution of the UK that a substantial constitutional change cannot be made (and therefore cannot be adopted) unless such a proposal has been approved by the electorate either as a result of the proposal being included in the manifesto of the party returned to government or in a referendum.	There is no seriously arguable case that a court will determine that an Act of Parliament passed without first having been the subject of a referendum or being included in a party manifesto will for that reason be unenforceable as a matter of law. There is nothing to substantiate that such a convention has the force of law.
Reference re Amendment to the Constitution of Canada (1982) 125 DLR (3rd) 385	In 1980, the Canadian Federal Government devised a package of Constitutional reforms which were opposed by a majority of the provinces. The Supreme Court of Canada was asked to decide whether the Federal Government could go ahead with the scheme without the consent of the provinces.	The courts have jurisdiction to determine whether a constitutional convention exists by asking: 1. what are the precedents; 2. do the actors in the precedents believe that they are bound by the rule; and is there a good reason for the rule?

Topic	'Do Constitutional Conventions Bind?'
Author/ Academic	Joseph Jaconelli.
Viewpoint	Examines the nature of the moral obligations that confer a binding force on constitutional conventions. Discusses the conceptual differences between constitutional conventions and constitutional law, and considers the arguments that have been put forward as to how this gap may be bridged. Assesses the validity of the objections that have been raised against the obligatory nature of constitutional conventions, and compares the basis for this purported obligatory force with that which applies to promises.
Source	(2005) 64(1) CLJ 149–176.

Topic	'The Robustness of Conventions in a Time of Modernization and Change'
Author/ Academic	Lord Wilson of Dinton
Viewpoint	Transcribes the text of the Harry Street Memorial Lecture given in Manchester on 17 October 2003, concerning the challenges posed to the UK's unwritten constitutional conventions. Discusses the scope of such conventions, their distinctiveness from constitutional practice and the pressures they face from media power, constitutional change, management reforms in the civil service, and public ignorance. Analyses the constitutional issues behind claims that the Prime Minister's role is becoming increasingly 'presidential' and comments on the potential dangers of the changing conventions of accountability and collective responsibility, highlighting the scope for confusion or unfairness towards civil servants and the importance of the distinction between accountability to Parliament and personal responsibility.
Source	[2004] PL 407–420.

Topic	'Laws and Constitutional Conventions'
Author/ Academic	NW Barber
Viewpoint	Examines the jurisdiction of the court in relation to constitutional conventions and the extent to which the courts are prepared to recognize them.
Source	(2009) Law Quarterly Review 294.

Exam questions

✱✱✱✱✱✱✱✱✱✱

Topic	'The 2010 General Election outcome and formation of the Conservative-Liberal Democrat coalition government'
Author/ Academic	Robert Blackburn
Viewpoint	Reflects on the formation and constitutional significance of the formation of the coalition government and relevant constitutional conventions.
Source	(2011, January) PL 2011, 30–55.

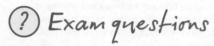 ⑦ Exam questions

Problem question

Assume that the Government loses a vote of no confidence following a debate in the House of Commons. The reason for this is that a large number of MPs were unable to attend the House of Commons because of exceptionally bad weather.

The Prime Minister refuses to resign. His argument is that the Government has a clear majority in the House of Commons and that had the MPs affected by the weather been able to get to Westminster, the Government would have won the vote of no confidence The leader of the Opposition argues that this is nonsense and that the Prime Minister and the Government should resign.

Advise the Queen's Private Secretary on the constitutional issues involved and the Leader of the Opposition as to whether he may take legal action to force the Prime Minister and the Government to resign.

Outline answers are included at the end of the book.

Essay question

Explain how and to what extent legal rules are enforceable in the courts and constitutional conventions are not.

 Scan here

Scan this QR code image with your mobile device to see an outline answer to this question or log onto www.oxfordtextbooks.co.uk/orc/concentrate

#3

The rule of law

Key Facts

- AV Dicey's conception of the **rule of law** is widely accepted.

- AV Dicey formulated the rule of law around the supremacy of law over arbitrary and wide discretionary power, equal subjection to the law and origins of constitutional law in private law.

- Dicey's views were based on the constitutional principles in **Entick v Carrington** (1765).

- Government according to law is an important principle connected with Dicey's conception of the rule of law.

- Jennings and others have put forward different views about what the rule of law means.

- Government according to law is a principle connected with the rule of law.

- There are examples of wide discretionary powers within the law of the United Kingdom which appear to run contrary to Dicey.

- There are other recognizable limitations and threats to the rule of law.

The meaning of the rule of law

- AV Dicey, in *Introduction to the Study of the Law of the Constitution* (1885), said that the **rule of law** means three things.

Firstly it means the predominance of law in preference to the influence of wide discretionary arbitrary prerogative power. This part of Dicey's definition also says that a person can be punished for a breach of the law and nothing else. Lord Bingham in the House of Lords' decision in *R v Rimmington; R v Goldstein* (2006) said that conduct forbidden by law should be clearly indicated so that a person is capable of knowing that it is wrong before he does it and that no one should be punished for doing something which was not a criminal offence when it was done.

Secondly, it means that everyone is equally subject to the law. According to Lord Bingham and Lord Walker in the Privy Council decision in *Sharma v Brown-Antoine and others* (2007) the rule of law requires that, subject to any immunity or exemption provided by law, the criminal law should apply to all alike. A person is not to be singled out for adverse treatment because he or she holds a high and dignified office of state, but nor can the holding of such an office excuse conduct which would lead to the prosecution of one not holding such an office. The maintenance of public confidence in the administration of justice requires that the law be even-handed.

The third part of Dicey's definition declares that the principles of British constitutional law do not, as in other countries, originate in a higher constitutional code. They come from the ordinary law which determines the rights and obligations of private individuals. Moreover, the law defining and governing the powers and liabilities of the Crown is an extension of the principles governing interpersonal rights and obligations in private law.

Jennings on Dicey

Sir Ivor Jennings, in *The Law and the Constitution*, 5th edn (1959), critically reviewed Dicey's conception of the rule of law. Jennings' main criticism of Dicey's views is that his preference for liberty, certainty, and the limitation of discretionary powers was inconsistent with twentieth century ideas of social justice, which involved the extension of discretionary powers. Jennings believed that the legal concept of the rule of law should have some key features. The state as a whole must be regulated by law. There must an implicit separation of powers. Police powers must be clearly defined. There must be clear general rules interpreted and applied by the courts. Criminal statutes should not be retrospective and should be interpreted strictly. Equality and liberty are also essential features of the rule of law.

Other views about what the rule of law means

There are many other views about what the rule of law means.

Joseph Raz, in *The Authority of Law* (1979), advances the view that the rule of law can be formulated as any political ideal to be realized in legal terms. This means that even a totalitarian regime may claim to have a 'rule of law'.

Friedrich Von Hayek, in *The Road to Serfdom* (1980), said that the rule of law means that government in all its action is bound by rules fixed and announced beforehand. He went on to say that these rules make it possible to foresee with fair certainty how the authority will use its coercive powers in given circumstances, and to plan one's individual affairs on the basis of this knowledge.

✅ Looking for extra marks?

Some essay type questions will ask you to compare and contrast different views about what the rule of law means. You should read your recommended standard textbook. Hilaire Barnett's textbook, *Constitutional and Administrative Law* (2006), contains a particularly good chapter on the rule of law and you should read this.

The key features of a legal system based on the rule of law

The following assertions have been made by judges concerning the key features of a legal system based on the rule of law. A decision to punish an offender with imprisonment may only be made by a court of law (Lord Steyn in *R (on the application of Anderson) v Secretary of State for the Home Department* (2003)). Civil rights must be determined by an independent and impartial judicial system (Lord Hoffmann in *Matthews v Ministry of Defence* (2003)). The executive should not arbitrarily be able to instruct the court to dismiss a claimant's action either by saying that there is no cause of action without the Government's consent or by issuing a certificate that the action is not to proceed (Lord Hoffmann in *Matthews v Ministry of Defence* (2003)). Judges preserve the rule of law. Common law rules governing access to the judicial system and judicial review form the cornerstone of the rule of law. Judges must interpret any statute which potentially threatens the rule of law so that it will not achieve this end. These points were laid down by Lord Philips MR in *R (on the application of G) v Immigration Appeal Tribunal; R (on the application of M) v Immigration Appeal Tribunal* (2005).

The constitutional principle of the rule of law was recognized by s 1 **Constitutional Reform Act 2005**, which provides that the Act does not adversely affect the constitutional principle of the rule of law.

The effect of the Human Rights Act 1998

The effect of the **Human Rights Act 1998** on the constitutional principle of the rule of law was discussed by Laws LJ in *R (on the application of Al Rawi and others) v Secretary of State for Foreign and Commonwealth Affairs and another* (2007). He said that because of statutes like the **1998 Act** the rule of law had become a more substantive principle: a public decision should be authorized by the words of an enabling statute and public authorities should make decisions which are both reasonable and proportionate to a legitimate aim.

Government according to law

> ### Revision tip
> You should be able to identify and state the principles of constitutional law upon which Dicey based his definition of the rule of law.

The constitutional principle in *Entick v Carrington* **(1765)** is the basis for some of Dicey's views about government according to law.

··

Entick v Carrington (1765) 95 ER 807.

In deciding that a warrant issued by the Secretary of State to enter and search the claimant's premises and seize property was illegal the Court of King's Bench determined that the executive can do nothing without legal authority. Where a public body claims to have the power to do something it must be able to identify the precise legal source of its powers.

··

✅ Looking for extra marks?

Some examination questions ask students to explain how the rule of law has been applied in English law in practice. You should be able to compare and contrast the views of senior members of the judiciary.

The key features of government according to law

Public bodies exercising statutory duties must do what the statute requires them to do as was held by Lord Goddard CJ in *Stroud v Bradbury* **(1952)**. The courts are duty bound to correct any abuse of power by the executive and the judges are free to exercise this jurisdiction independently. This was determined by Lord Denning in *Congreve v Home Office* **(1976)**. The judiciary enforces the law against individuals, institutions, and the executive. Judges cannot enforce the law against the monarch because the monarch can do no wrong but judges enforce the law against the executive and against the individuals who from time to time represent the executive. A litigant complaining of a breach of the law by the executive can sue the Crown as executive bringing his action against the minister who is responsible for the department of state involved. To enforce the law the courts have power to grant remedies against a minister in his official capacity. If a minister has personally broken the law, the litigant can sue the minister in his personal capacity. For the purpose of enforcing the law against all persons and institutions, including ministers in their official capacity, the courts are armed with coercive powers exercisable in proceedings for contempt of court. These points were made in Lord Templeman's speech in *M v Home Office* **(1993)**.

Lord Mustill, in his dissenting speech in *R v Secretary of State for the Home Department, ex p the Firebrigades' Union* **(1995)**, said that the role of the courts is to make sure that powers are lawfully exercised by those to whom they are entrusted, not to take those powers into their own hands and exercise them afresh. He concluded that a claim that a decision under challenge is wrong leads nowhere, except in the rare cases where it can be characterized as so obviously and grossly wrong as to be irrational, in the lawyer's sense of the word, and hence a symptom that there must have been some failure in the decision-making process.

Threats to the constitutional principle of the rule of law

Revision Tip

You may be asked in an examination question to assess the continuing value or even the true existence of the rule of law today. You should acquaint yourself with current debates.

Arbitrary and wide discretionary powers

A statutory provision that a public body *may* do something *if/as they see fit* or *if they reasonably believe* something is a subjective discretionary power. Such discretion can be both wide and arbitrary. Can the courts intervene and, if so, how far? In *Liversidge v Anderson* (1942) the House of Lords said that under normal circumstances, the judges are 'no respecters of persons'. They stand between the citizen and any attempted encroachments on his liberty. They particularly ensure that coercive action is justified by law. But, in times of emergency, arbitrary and wide subjective discretionary powers are permitted.

Even in times of peace subjective discretion can be given to the executive. **Section 3(5)(a) Immigration Act 1971** provides that a person may be deported if the Secretary of State 'deems' his deportation to be conducive to the public good. **Section 21(1) Anti-terrorism, Crime and Security Act 2001** provides that a person could be deported if the Secretary of State reasonably believes that the person's presence in the United Kingdom is a risk to national security, and suspects that person is a terrorist.

The provisions of the **Immigration Act 1971**, as amended by the **British Nationality Act 1981** were considered by the House of Lords in *Secretary of State for the Home Department v Rehman* (2003).

The House of Lords had to consider whether it was necessary to engage in, promote, or encourage violent activity targeted at the United Kingdom, its system of government, or its people and whether a high degree of probability that the applicant had been, was, or was likely to be a threat to national security was necessary before a decision to deport was made by the Secretary of State.

The House of Lords made four essential points. The first is that what is conducive to the public good is a matter for the executive discretion of the Secretary of State. Secondly, the Secretary of State is entitled to take an overall view. Thirdly, the interests of national security can be threatened not only by action against the United Kingdom but also indirectly by activities directed against other states. Fourthly, while any specific facts on which the Secretary of State relies must be proved on the ordinary civil balance of probability, no particular standard of proof is appropriate to the formation of his executive judgment or assessment as to whether it is conducive to the public good that a person be deported, which is a matter of reasonable and proportionate judgment. The **Terrorism Act 2005** extends these powers.

Issues relating to the courts' power to scrutinize wide discretionary powers were discussed by the House of Lords in *A and Others v Secretary of State for the Home Department* (2005). Lord Nicholls identified and stated the following. Indefinite imprisonment without charge is contrary to the rule of law because it deprives the detained person of the protection given to them by the process of criminal trial. The primary burden of protecting national security rests with the executive. The executive's role is to evaluate and decide upon appropriate anti-terrorist measures. The role of the judiciary, in a legal system based on the rule of law, is to make sure that legislation and ministerial decisions do not overlook the human rights of those adversely affected and that both Parliament and the executive give due weight to fundamental rights and freedoms. In carrying out its role, the judiciary will give both Parliament and the executive an appropriate degree of latitude. The degree of latitude given will depend upon the nature of the matter being considered, the importance of the human right in question and the extent of the encroachment upon the right. The courts will intervene only when it is apparent that, in balancing the various considerations involved, the primary decision-maker must have given insufficient weight to the human rights factor.

Laws LJ in *R (on the application of Al Rawi and others) v Secretary of State for Foreign and Commonwealth Affairs and another* (2007) accepted Lord Hoffmann's views in *Secretary of State for the Home Department v Rehman* (2003) for judicial non-intervention in the process of executive decision-making. Judicial non-intervention is justified where the executive has access to special information and expertise and a decision, because of its nature and consequences, requires such legitimacy that it can be made only by a person accountable to Parliament and the electorate.

Subsequently, *R (Corner House Research) v Director of the Serious Fraud Office* (2009) it was recognized that the rule of law is not absolute. National security, as well as other public interest considerations, can outweigh the Dicean injunction forbidding wide discretionary and arbitrary powers.

Privileges, immunities, and the rule of law

Revision tip

Another important and examinable aspect of the rule of law is the question of whether special powers, privileges, and immunities conferred by statute can be reconciled with Dicey's view of the rule of law.

Figure 3.1 The executive and judiciary's role within the rule of law

The Executive	The Judiciary
Takes primary responsibility for enacting legislation and decision-making.	Makes sure that legislation and Ministerial decisions do not overlook legal formalities and the Human Rights of those adversely affected.
May evaluate and decide upon appropriate measures.	Gives both Parliament and the executive a degree of latitude.
	The degree of latitude depends on the nature of the matter being considered, the importance of the human rights in question and the extent of the encroachment.
	The courts will intervene only when it is apparent that, in balancing the various considerations involved, the primary decision-maker must have given insufficient weight to the human rights factor.

Special powers, privileges, and immunities from the ordinary law have been granted by Parliament, so that it is possible to argue that the principle of equal subjection to the law is undermined. **Article 9 Bill of Rights 1689** gives absolute immunity to MPs from actions in the tort of defamation arising out of anything said or done in the course of a parliamentary debate or parliamentary proceeding. The **International Organisations Act 2005** enables the UK to fulfil international commitments to confer legal capacity and privileges and immunities on a number of international organizations and bodies, and certain categories of individuals connected to them. Trade unions enjoy some immunities under the **Trade Union and Labour Relations (Consolidation) Act 1992**. The **Diplomatic Privileges Act 1964** is another example.

The extension of the criminal law by the judiciary

Revision tip

This is another area where Dicey's conception of the rule of law may be called into question. When revising this part of the topic you should, first, read Lord Simonds' speech in *Shaw v DPP* (1962) and then compare this with Lord Reid's opinion in the same case.

Because Dicey said that 'a man may with us be punished for a breach of law, but he can be punished for nothing else', the courts should not be able to create or extend criminal offences. This issue was addressed by the House of Lords in the following case:

....

Shaw v DPP [1962] AC 220

Shaw published a Ladies Directory containing the names and addresses of prostitutes. He was charged, among other things, with conspiracy to corrupt public morals in that he conspired with the advertisers and other persons by means of the 'Ladies Directory' and the advertisements to debauch and corrupt the morals of youth and other subjects of the Queen. He was convicted. He appealed on the ground that there was no such offence as conspiracy to corrupt public morals. The case reached the House of Lords. Speaking for the majority, Lord Simonds claimed that there was a residual judicial power to enforce the supreme and fundamental purpose of the law. The purpose of the law, according to Lord Simonds, was to protect the safety, order, and moral welfare of the state. He concluded that the courts had a duty to protect the state against novel and unexpected attacks. Lord Reid dissented on the ground that it was contrary to the rule of law for the courts to create or extend criminal offences on public policy grounds.

In the House of Lords' decision in *R v Rimmington; R v Goldstein* **(2006)**, Lord Bingham said that if the ambit of a common law offence is to be enlarged, it must be done step by step, on a case-by-case basis and not with one large leap.

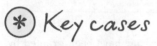 (✱) **Key cases**

Case	Facts	Principle
***A and Others v Secretary of State for the Home Department* [2005] 2 AC 68**	The House of Lords had to decide on the legality of certain anti-terrorist measures.	Indefinite imprisonment without charge is contrary to the rule of law because it deprives the detained person of the protection given to them by the process of criminal trial. The role of the judiciary, in a legal system based on the rule of law, is to make sure that legislation and ministerial decisions do not overlook the human rights of those adversely affected. In carrying out its role, the judiciary will give both Parliament and the executive an appropriate degree of latitude, which will depend upon: the nature of the matter being considered; the importance of the human right in question; and the extent of the encroachment upon the right. The courts will intervene only when it is apparent that, in balancing the various considerations involved, the primary decision-maker must have given insufficient weight to the human rights factor.
***Entick v Carrington* (1765) St Tr 1029**	The Court of King's Bench had to decide whether national security could be raised as a defence to an action in trespass to land and property.	The executive can do nothing without legal authority. Where a public authority claims to have the power to do something it must be able to identify the precise legal source of its powers.

Case	Facts	Principle
M v Home Office [1993] 3 WLR 433	Proceedings were brought against the Home Secretary for contempt of Court. The House of Lords determined that the courts had jurisdiction.	The judiciary enforce the law against individuals, institutions, the executive, and against the individuals who from time to time represent the executive. A litigant complaining of a breach of the law by the executive can sue the Crown as executive bringing his action against the minister who is responsible for the department of state involved. The courts have power to grant remedies against a minister in his official capacity. If a minister has personally broken the law, the litigant can sue the minister in his personal capacity. The courts are armed with coercive powers exercisable in proceedings for contempt of court.
R v Secretary of State for the Home Department, ex p the Firebrigades' Union [1995] All ER 244	The House of Lords had to decide whether the Home Secretary had acted lawfully in the way he had dealt with the implementation of a scheme to provide compensation to the victims of violent crime.	The courts ensure that powers are lawfully exercised by those to whom they are entrusted, not to take those powers into their own hands and exercise them afresh. A claim that a decision under challenge is wrong leads nowhere, except in the rare cases where it can be characterized as so obviously and grossly wrong as to be irrational, in the lawyer's sense of the word, and hence a symptom that there must have been some failure in the decision-making process.
Secretary of State for the Home Department v Rehman [2001] 3 WLR 877	The applicant, a Pakistani, arrived in the United Kingdom in 1993 after being granted entry clearance to work as a minister of religion. In December 1998 the Secretary of State refused his application for indefinite leave to remain in the United Kingdom and gave notice that, because of his association with an organization involved in terrorist activities in India, he had decided to make a deportation order under s 3(5)(b) Immigration Act 1971 on the ground that it would be conducive to the public good and in the interests of national security.	What is conducive to the public good is a matter for the executive discretion of the Secretary of State. The Secretary of State is entitled to take an overall view. The interests of national security can be threatened not only by action against the United Kingdom but also indirectly by activities directed against other states. While any specific facts on which the Secretary of State relies must be proved on the ordinary civil balance of probability, no particular standard of proof is appropriate to the formation of his executive judgment or assessment as to whether it is conducive to the public good that a person be deported, which is a matter of reasonable and proportionate judgment.

Key debates

****

Key debates

Topic	'The launch of the Bingham Centre for the Rule of Law'
Name/Academic	Jeffrey Jowell and Roger Errera
Viewpoint	Provides extracts from speeches delivered at the launch of the Bingham Centre for the Rule of Law on 6 December 2010. Includes discussion of the historical development of the rule of law from the mid-twentieth century, the role of the **Constitutional Reform Act 2005**, and the aims of the Centre.
Source	(2011) European Human Rights Law Review 1 1–4.

Topic	'Two Models of Constitutionalism and the Legitimacy of Law: Dicey or Marshall?'
Author/Academic	Luc B Tremblay
Viewpoint	Compares American constitutionalism associated with Chief Justice Marshall's reasoning in *Marbury v Madison* **(1803)** with the British constitutionalism expounded by Albert Dicey in *Introduction to the Study of the Law of the Constitution*. Considers how the rules and principles of constitutional law are conceived as the source of government action in the American model and as the consequence of government action in the British model. Argues that the British model is superior from a descriptive and normative point of view.
Source	(2006) 6(1) Oxford University Commonwealth Law Journal 77–101.

Topic	'Parliamentary Sovereignty under the New Constitutional Hypothesis'
Author/Academic	Jeffrey Jowell
Viewpoint	Identifies two possible justifications for limiting parliamentary sovereignty: legitimacy and the changing hypothesis of constitutionalism, based primarily on the judicial review of administrative action.
Source	[2006] PL 562–580.

Topic	'Questioning Common Law Constitutionalism'
Author/Academic	Thomas Poole
Viewpoint	Analyses the theory of common law constitutionalism and the role of judicial review in assessing the legitimacy of governmental action. Considers the relationship between common law constitutionalism and the debate over the viability of ultra vires. Explores whether there exists a unified theory, the main features of common law constitutionalism, and the nature of judicial review within a common law constitution.
Source	(2005) 25(1) Legal Studies 142–163.

Topic	'The Rule of Law as the Rule of Reason: Consent and Constitutionalism'
Author/Academic	TRS Allan
Viewpoint	Critique of Joseph Raz's theory that rule of law should not be limited purely to the idea of formal legality but should include elements of social justice.
Source	(1999) 115 Law Quarterly Review 221–244.

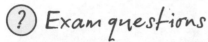 Exam questions

Essay question 1

Explain Dicey's conception of the rule of law.

Essay question 2

Explain the extent to which, if at all, Dicey's conception of the rule of law is of value today.

 Scan here

Scan this QR code image with your mobile device to see outline answers to these questions or log onto www.oxfordtextbooks.co.uk/orc/concentrate

#4

The separation of powers

Key Facts

- There are three functions of government, namely, the legislative function, the executive function, and the judicial function.

- There are three corresponding organs of government, namely, the legislature, the executive, and the judiciary.

- In its present form, 'separation of powers' was first formulated by Montesquieu, and was partly based on the writings of John Locke.

- The same persons should not form part of more than one of the three organs of government.

- One organ of government should not exercise the functions of another.

- Each organ of government should act as a check against the other and should be able to do this independently without any undue threat of preventative control or interference.

- The separation of powers is mentioned in the opinions of judges in decided cases and is supported by statutes like the **Constitutional Reform Act 2005**.

- A detailed analysis of the structure of and interrelationship between the functions and organs of the UK Government reveals that the 'British Constitution' departs from the principle of 'separation of powers' in many vital respects especially at the higher levels.

Revision tip

This topic links up closely with the rule of law, sovereignty of Parliament, and human rights. Examination questions frequently mix separation of powers with these subjects. For this reason this topic should not be revised in isolation.

The functions of government

Revision tip

The separation of powers assumes that government is based on three recognized functions. When examining the legal concept of the separation of powers you should have a clear idea of the nature and extent of the functions of government. See chapters 5, 6, and 7.

There are three functions of government and three corresponding organs of government. The three functions of government are executive, legislative, and judicial.

The legislative function

This is the law-making function. It provides the necessary machinery to make, unmake, or amend the law. See chapter 7.

The executive function

This is the administrative function. It enforces the law, maintains order, promotes social and economic welfare, manages public services, conducts the external relations of the state, forms policy, initiates legislation, and manages routine services.

See also chapter 6.

The judicial function

The primary judicial function is to interpret and apply the law, resolve disputes, provide remedies, and determine punishments when the law is breached. The judiciary consists of all judges who preside in the senior and lower courts within the United Kingdom.

The corresponding three organs of government are the Legislature, Executive, and Judiciary.

The separation of powers

Revision tip

It is important to understand how the separation of powers is formulated as both a political and a legal principle.

The meaning of the separation of powers

At a basic level the 'separation of powers' means that the same persons should not form part of more than one of the three organs of government, one organ of government should not exercise the functions of another, and each organ of government should act as a check against the others and should be able to do this independently without any undue threat of preventative control or interference.

This was first developed by John Locke in his *Second Treatise of Civil Government* in 1690. It was developed further by Montesquieu in his book *De l'Esprit des Lois* in 1748.

Separation of powers and the common law

Revision tip

As with the rule of law you should be able to compare, contrast, and assess the judicial appreciation of the separation of powers.

The separation of powers is mentioned in the speeches and judgments of senior members of the judiciary in decided cases. In the House of Lords' decision in *Duport Steels Ltd v Sirs* (1980) Lord Diplock said that the British Constitution is firmly based on the separation of powers in that Parliament makes the laws and the judiciary interprets them. In this case, the separation of powers was used to draw a distinction between the legislative and judicial functions with a view to keeping the judiciary within bounds.

In the House of Lords' decision in *M v Home Office* (1993) Lord Templeman emphasized that Parliament makes the laws, the executive carries the laws into effect, and the judiciary enforces them.

The separation of powers was discussed in the dissenting speech of Lord Mustill in *R v Secretary of State for the Home Department, ex parte Fire Brigades Union* (1995). He said that Parliament, the executive, and the courts each have their distinct and largely exclusive domain. He went on to say that Parliament has a largely unchallengeable right to make whatever laws it thinks right. The executive carries on the administration of the country and the courts interpret the laws and sees that they are obeyed.

The Constitutional Reform Act 2005 and the separation of powers

Some statutes, like the **Constitutional Reform Act 2005**, support the separation of powers. The Act imposes a duty on government ministers to uphold the independence of the judiciary. Members of the executive cannot influence judicial decisions and do not have any special right of access to judges. The judicial functions of the Lord Chancellor were transferred to the President of the Courts of England and Wales. He now represents the views of the judiciary to the executive and takes responsibility for the training, guidance, and deployment of judges. The executive functions of the Lord Chancellor are now carried out by the Secretary of State for Justice who heads the Ministry of Justice. The parliamentary functions of the Lord Chancellor are now carried out by the Lord Speaker of the House of Lords. The Act established the Supreme Court of the United Kingdom, which took over the work of the Appellate Committee of the House of Lords in October 2009. The jurisdiction of the Judicial Committee of the Privy Council was devolved. Furthermore, the Act created the Judicial Appointments Commission, which is responsible for selecting candidates to recommend for judicial appointment on merit and in an open and transparent manner. It also created the Judicial Appointments and Conduct Ombudsman, responsible for investigating and making recommendations concerning complaints about the judicial appointments process, and the handling of judicial conduct complaints.

To what extent is the government of the United Kingdom truly based on the separation of powers?

The relationship between the executive and Parliament

Revision tip

This is a very commonly examined aspect of the separation of powers and you should be prepared to follow up this topic in the standard textbooks. This part of the topic links up with human rights and sovereignty of Parliament and should be revised in conjunction with those topics. When you revise the topics set out in chapters 5, 6, 7, 8, and 14 you should bear in mind the separation of powers implications.

In terms of legal formality the monarch, as the head of state, is the head of the executive, the legislature, and the judiciary. The Prime Minister, the members of the Cabinet, and all the other ministers of the Crown are members of the executive. They are also Members of Parliament. If the organs and functions of government within the United Kingdom were organized strictly according the doctrine of separation of powers the Prime Minister, the members of the Cabinet, and all the other ministers of the Crown would not be permitted to be members of Parliament.

The monarch too would not be permitted to be part of the legislature or have any part to play in the appointment of judges.

Two statutes seek to limit the extent to which the executive can control the legislature. The first is **s 2** of the **House of Commons (Disqualification) Act 1975, which** limits the number of ministers appointed from the membership of the House of Commons to 95. The result, as far as the separation of powers is concerned, is that it is impossible for the House of Commons to be completely composed of members of the executive. The second is **s 18** and **Sch 6** of the

The separation of powers

****

Constitutional Reform Act 2005, which divided the duties of the Lord Chancellor between the Secretary of State for Justice, who is now a member of the House of Commons, and the Speaker of the House of Lords. The Lord Chancellor's Department was replaced by the Ministry of Justice.

Some statutes appear to reinforce a very close relationship between the legislature and the executive. These include the **Regulatory Reform Act 2001**, as amended by the **Legislative and Regulatory Reform Act 2006**, which enable a minister of the Crown to make orders for the purpose of amending certain categories of provisions in statutes. These categories are stipulated in the **2001** and **2006 Acts**. Moreover **s 10 Human Rights Act 1998** enables Ministers of the Crown to make remedial orders amending legislation which is incompatible with human rights incorporated by the **1998 Act**.

Other statutes allow ministers and local authorities to make laws. These may take the form of Orders in Council, Statutory Instruments, Regulations, Rules, Orders, Schemes, Warrants, By Laws, and Directions – Acts of Parliament which create such powers are called primary legislation. The regulations created under them are called delegated legislation.

Different perspectives on the relationship between the legislature and the executive

Walter Bagehot, in *The English Constitution* (1876), said that there was a close union or fusion of the executive and legislative powers in the British system of government. He did not see this as a bad thing: it actually made the government work better. LS Amery, in *Thoughts on the Constitution* (1948), on the other hand, emphasized the different and distinct functions of the executive and the legislature: the executive leads, directs, and commands; the legislature provides a forum for critical debate, consultation, and accountability. However closely the executive and legislature work together, these separate and distinct functions cannot be ignored. Neither can their separate origins and methods.

Lord Hailsham, in *The Dilemma of Democracy: Diagnosis and Prescription* (1978), called the British system of government an elective dictatorship. He begins by considering the doctrine which gives Parliament absolute and unlimited legislative powers. The question is whether this doctrine ought to be modified because of changes in the way Parliament is structured and operates. The basis of his argument is that there has been a continuous enlargement of executive power and a corresponding decline of parliamentary influence. All effective powers are placed in the hands of the executive and the checks and balances, which in practice used to prevent abuse, have now disappeared. Another major factor is the development of the **whip system**. Whips are MPs or Lords appointed by each party in Parliament to help organize their party's contribution to parliamentary business. One of their responsibilities is making sure the maximum number of their party members vote, and vote the way their party wants. In Lord Hailsham's opinion this gives the whips, party leaders, and the executive the power to control Parliament and suppress the debate and argument which once dominated the parliamentary scene. He concludes that elective dictatorship is a fact and not just a lawyer's theory.

The relationship between the executive and the judiciary

This was explained fully by Lord Mustill in *R v Secretary of State for the Home Department ex p Fire Brigades Union* (1995). He said that the role of the judiciary in relation to the executive was to verify that the powers asserted accord with the substantive law created by Parliament, and also to ensure that the manner in which they are exercised conforms with the standards of fairness which Parliament must have intended.

The judiciary and the executive: Is the judiciary really independent?

Revision tip

Again, this should be revised in conjunction with human rights and sovereignty of Parliament.

An independent judiciary is essential to the separation of powers. This is illustrated by two decisions of the House of Lords. The first case is *R (on the application of Anderson) v Secretary of State for the Home Department* (2003). Here, Lord Steyn restated the principle, linked to both the rule of law and the separation of powers, that a decision to punish an offender with a term of imprisonment should be made by the courts. The only recognized exception is the ancient power of Parliament to imprison those who are held to be in contempt of Parliament. This is based on the medieval principle that Parliament may act as a court of justice. The second case is *Matthews v Ministry of Defence* (2003). Here, the House said that the executive must never be put in a position where it effectively decides a case in the sense that it could order a court to dismiss a case. What matters is whether the effect of a legal provision is to give the executive a right to make decisions about people's rights which should be made by the judicial branch of government.

Section 3(1) Constitutional Reform Act 2005 provides that the Lord Chancellor, other ministers of the Crown, and all with responsibility for matters relating to the judiciary or otherwise to the administration of justice must uphold the continued independence of the judiciary.

The appointment of judges

Judges are legally appointed by the monarch on the advice of ministers. The question is whether the judiciary can be really independent if the judges are all appointed by the executive. Following the **Constitutional Reform Act 2005** two important developments in the way judges are appointed have separation of powers implications. Firstly, the **Constitutional Reform Act 2005** created a new appointments process for Justices of the UK Supreme Court. New justices are selected by a selection commission, the members of which include the President and Deputy President of the Supreme Court, a member of the Judicial Appointments Commission of England and Wales, the Judicial Appointments Board for Scotland, and the Northern Ireland Judicial Appointments Commission. Secondly, the **2005 Act** created the Judicial Appointments Commission which selects new judges in the senior courts. Both these measures were designed to reinforce the independence of the judiciary.

The dismissal of judges

Judges cannot be dismissed summarily by the executive. The **Act of Settlement 1700** and the **Senior Courts Act 1981** provide that judges hold office 'during good behaviour' and cannot be removed from office without the permission of both Houses of Parliament. This takes the form of a petition to the reigning monarch.

The Civil Procedure Rule Committee

The Civil Procedure Rule Committee is an advisory non-departmental public body set up under the **Civil Procedure Act 1997** to make rules of court for the Civil Division of the Court of Appeal, the High Court, and the county courts. As such, it is part of the executive and provides the executive with a role in the development of civil procedure. The issue here is whether the executive could influence the development of civil procedure in its favour. On the other hand, the committee is largely staffed by members of the judiciary and the legal profession, which alleviates the problem to a large extent.

The relationship between the courts and Parliament

The *sub judice* 'rule' prevents the discussion of ongoing cases in Parliament, but, subject to that, the decisions and conduct of individual Judges may be mentioned in debates in either House of Parliament. This does not, however, mean that judges are accountable to Parliament for their decisions in particular cases.

Parliament may legislate to reverse the effect of a decision or change the law as established or interpreted by a judicial decision. An example of this is the **War Damage Act 1965** which immediately followed the decision of the House of Lords' judgment in *Burmah Oil Co Ltd v Lord Advocate* (1965) and took effect retrospectively to reverse the House of Lords' decision that Burmah Oil Co Ltd was entitled to compensation for war damage suffered in 1942. Another example is the **Terrorist Asset Freezing (Temporary Provisions) Act 2010**. This Act, which was repealed by the **Terrorist Asset Freezing Act 2010**, was rapidly passed following the decision of the UK Supreme Court in **HM Treasury v Ahmed (2010)** not to suspend orders to quash two Orders in Council because they were incompatible with the **United Nations Act 1946**. The Act said that the orders in question were validly adopted according to the provisions of the **United Nations Act 1946**. It retained in force all the directions made under those orders.

Figure 4.1

No separation of powers	
The Monarch	Titular head of the executive, legislative, and judicial functions and organs of government.
The Privy Council & Cabinet	Exercises executive, legislative, and judicial powers and contains members of each organ of government.
Partial separation of powers	
Legislature	Contains members of the judiciary and the executive but the executive's hold limited by statute.
Executive	Under the supervision of the legislature and the judiciary but can exercise considerable power over the legislature through the whip system. See Lord Hailsham's views on the elective dictatorship.
Judiciary	Organizationally independent but subject to Parliamentary sovereignty.

 **Key cases**

Case	Facts	Principle
Duport Steels Ltd v Sirs [1980] 1 All ER 529	The House of Lords had to decide whether it was appropriate to grant an injunction to restrain secondary picketing on the ground that it was not covered by statutory immunities concerning trade union action as part of a trade dispute.	The British Constitution is firmly based on the separation of powers in that Parliament makes the laws and the judiciary interpret them.
Matthews v Ministry of Defence [2003] 1 AC 1163	This was a negligence claim involving considerations of Article 6 European Convention on Human Rights and Fundamental Freedoms.	The executive must never be put in a position where it effectively decides a case in the sense that it could order a court to dismiss a case. What matters is whether the effect of a legal provision is to give the executive a right to make decisions about people's rights which should be made by the judicial branch of government.

Key debates

✱✱✱✱✱✱✱✱✱✱✱✱

Case	Facts	Principle
R (on the application of Al Rawi and others) v Secretary of State for Foreign and Commonwealth Affairs and another [2007] 2 WLR 1219	The Court of Appeal had to decide whether the courts must review the substance of an executive decision in human rights cases.	The role of the executive is to make decisions where it has access to special information or expertise or where the nature and consequences of the decision require accountability to the legislature and to the electorate. The role of the judiciary is to make sure that the executive complies with all formal requirements, considers matters rationally, and makes decisions, especially where human rights issues are involved, in accordance with the principle of proportionality.
R v Secretary of State for the Home Department, ex p Fire Brigades Union [1995] 2 All ER 244	See chapter 3 on the rule of law.	Parliament, the executive, and the courts each have their distinct and largely exclusive domain. Parliament has a largely unchallengeable right to make whatever laws it thinks right. The executive carries on the administration of the country. The courts interpret the laws, and see that they are obeyed.

 **Key debates**

Topic	'The new UK Supreme Court, the separation of powers and anti-terrorism measures'
Author/Academic	Angus Johnston and Eva Nanopoulos
Viewpoint	Examines the Supreme Court decision in **HM Treasury v Ahmed** on whether the **Terrorism (United Nations Measures) Order 2006** and the **Al-Qaida and Taliban (United Nations Measures) Order 2006**, which gave effect to UN Security Council Resolutions ordering the freezing of the assets of terrorist suspects, were *ultra vires* the **United Nations Act 1946 s 1(1)** on the ground that they interfered with these suspects' human rights, an act that could only be authorized by Parliament. Assesses whether the Orders were measures were 'necessary or expedient' to enforce the UN decisions without prior parliamentary scrutiny or approval within the meaning of **s 1(1)**.
Source	(2010) Cambridge Law Journal 69(2), 217–220

Topic	'Judicial Activism in the House of Lords: A Composite Constitutionalist Approach'
Author/Academic	Margit Cohn
Viewpoint	Discusses the issue of judicial activism and the role of the judiciary, and notes Cohn and Kremnitzer's model of judicial activism. Presents a composite model of judicial activism and judicial restraint/deference.
Source	[2007] Public Law 95–115.

Topic	'Constitutionalism and the Abolition of the Lord Chancellor'
Author/Academic	Dawn Oliver
Viewpoint	Outlines the proposed changes to the administration of justice in the UK announced in June 2003.
Source	(2004) 57(4) Parliamentary Affairs 754–766.

Topic	'A Supreme Court for the United Kingdom: a note on early days'
Author/academic	Jo Lennan
Viewpoint	Outlines the legislative background to the creation of the UK Supreme Court in 2009, noting the extent of the jurisdiction transferred to it, reactions to its creation, and the nature of the matters it has dealt with in its first few months of existence. Discusses whether the creation of the Court was more than a formality and contemplates the effect which development of its jurisdiction to review devolution legislation could have on its willingness to review other legislation.
Source	(2010) 29(2) Civil Justice Quarterly 139–145

Topic	'Constitutional Reforms, the Supreme Court, and the Law Lords'
Author/Academic	Lord Mance
Viewpoint	Comments on the background to the constitutional reforms involving the abolition of the Lord Chancellor's Department and the creation of a UK Supreme Court.
Source	(2006) 25 Civil Justice Quarterly 155–165.

Exam questions

Topic	'The Judges and the Executive – Have the Goalposts been Moved?'
Author/Academic	Lord Lloyd of Berwick
Viewpoint	Reproduces the text of the Denning Lecture 2005 on the relationship between the judiciary, the legislature, and the executive.
Source	[2006] Denning Law Journal 79–94.

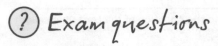 **Exam questions**

Essay question 1

Explain the functions and organs of government within the United Kingdom. What is meant by the separation of powers and what evidence is there that it is accepted as a legal principle?

Essay question 2

To what extent is the British system of government based on a fusion or separation of powers?

 Scan here

Scan this QR code image with your mobile device to see outline answers to these questions or log onto www.oxfordtextbooks.co.uk/orc/concentrate

#5

Constitutional monarchy and the royal prerogative

Key Facts

- The British Constitution is monarchical.

- The head of state of the United Kingdom of Great Britain and Northern Ireland is called the monarch, or the reigning king or queen.

- Three principles apply to the monarch as head of state namely, the monarch never dies, the monarch is never an infant, and the monarch can do no wrong.

- The legal source of the monarch's powers, as head of state, is the Royal Prerogative exercised in accordance with binding political rules and practices.

- Many Royal Prerogative powers have been delegated to the executive.

The head of state

Every country with an organized government has a head of state. There are different types of heads of state. Some are executive heads of state who actively exercise legal and political power and others are non-executive heads of state whose powers are purely legal and formal. They do not participate in the political process. Most heads of state are elected. Others, like the British monarch, take office under the hereditary principle.

The UK monarch as head of state

Revision tip

Having a clear idea of the constitutional role and powers of the monarch will help you to understand the context in which the Royal Prerogative has been delegated to members of the executive. This topic also links up with what you will be studying in chapters 6, 7, and 8. You should also bear in mind the separation of powers.

In its legal form the United Kingdom constitution is monarchical. The United Kingdom is a constitutional monarchy: the monarch exercises their legal powers as part of a system of government which is parliamentary and democratic. The reigning monarch is the head of state of the United Kingdom of Great Britain and Northern Ireland, Supreme Governor of the Church of England, Commander in Chief of the Army, Navy, and Air Force, nominal head of the judiciary, and head of the legislature.

The monarch is also head of state of his/her other Realms and Territories and Defender of the Faith.

When exercising their personal legal powers as head of state, the reigning monarch is sometimes referred to as the Crown or the Sovereign. The country in which a monarch performs their legal role as head of state is on some occasions called a kingdom or realm.

Special privileges and immunities of the monarch

Revision tip

Again, essay questions can focus on this topic. It also forms the background to what you will study in chapter 13. You should also refer to the key cases and key debates section at the end of this chapter for further material.

The monarch is never an infant

This primarily means that certain contracts made by the monarch before they reach the age of 18 are enforceable. Special guardianship rules apply to monarchs who are under the age of 18.

The monarch never dies

The death of a king or queen is legally called the demise of the sovereign. Upon the demise of the sovereign the heir to the throne can act as head of state immediately. He or she does not have to wait for the coronation ceremony.

The monarch can do no wrong

A monarch cannot be held legally accountable for their conduct as head of state or the consequences of decisions taken collectively by the Government or individually by ministers. At common law the courts have no jurisdiction over the monarch in person. This applies to civil and criminal proceedings. The monarch cannot be sued in their own courts. Two possible exceptions are a petition of right granted with the permission of the Attorney General and an action brought against the Attorney General for a declaration affecting the monarch's rights.

This immunity does not extend to other members of the royal family.

✅ Looking for extra marks?

In recent years a debate has emerged concerning reform of these principles. You should read, especially, 'Crown Immunity from Criminal Liability in English Law' [2003] PL 716. in which Maurice Sunkin discusses the possible different meanings of 'the monarch can do no wrong' and the influence of statute.

The powers and duties of the monarch: the Royal Prerogative

Revision tip

Essay questions, in particular, may ask you to explain what the Royal Prerogative is, as well as its nature, scope, and justiciability. Going through the elements of Dicey's definition is a good way to begin your analysis.

The Royal Prerogative as a source of the monarch's powers

AV Dicey defined the Royal Prerogative as the residue of discretionary or arbitrary authority, which at any given time is legally left in the hands of the Crown. The Royal Prerogative is 'residual' in the sense that the judges will not add to the monarch's powers and that these powers can be taken away by statute, 'arbitrary' and 'discretionary' meaning that the monarch cannot be held accountable in the courts for the exercise of these powers, and applicable to the 'the Crown' meaning either the monarch or the executive.

The UK monarch as head of state
****

In the House of Lords' decision in *Attorney General v De Keyser's Royal Hotel Ltd* (1920) Lord Dunedin quoted and accepted AV Dicey's definition of the Royal Prerogative.

Prerogative powers, which the monarch exercises as head of state, include the appointment of the Prime Minister, dissolution of Parliament, Royal Assent, dismissal of ministers, appointments, and honours.

The conduct of foreign affairs, the signing of treaties, and the deployment of armed forces are also included. The prerogative also covers certain immunities such as the Crown not being bound by statute unless it is expressly provided or it is by necessary implication. The Royal Prerogative also includes the power to make Orders in Council. This is a type of subordinate legislation.

Revision tip

You will note that Dicey said that the Royal Prerogative is a 'residue'. One of the implications of this is that that the Royal Prerogative cannot be enlarged as a source of executive Power. Consideration of the following cases will help you understand this.

The Royal Prerogative and statute

There are two key principles. The first, which was laid down by the House of Lords in *Attorney-General v De Keyser's Royal Hotel Ltd* (1920), is that when a statute is passed it abridges the Royal Prerogative while the statute is in force so that the executive can act only under and in accordance with the statute. The executive is also bound by all the limitations, restrictions, and conditions imposed by the statute. The second, which was determined by the House of Lords in *R v Secretary of State for the Home Department, ex p Fire Brigades Union* (1995) is that it is an abuse of power for the executive to purport to use the Royal Prerogative to achieve something which is inconsistent with a statutory scheme and use the Royal Prerogative to frustrate the will of Parliament expressed in a statute so that it pre-empts a parliamentary decision on whether or not to do something.

Can the Royal Prerogative powers exercised by the monarch be subject to legal scrutiny?

In *Council of Civil Service Unions v Minister for the Civil Service (GCHQ)* (1984) the House of Lords said that executive action is not immune from **judicial review** merely because it is carried out in pursuance of a power derived from the Royal Prerogative. A minister exercising power under the Prerogative might, depending on the **justiciability** of its subject matter, be under the same duty to act fairly as in the case of action taken under a statutory power.

Concerning justiciability, Lord Roskill thought that, as well as others, the grant of honours, the dissolution of Parliament, the making of treaties, and the appointment of ministers were not open to legal scrutiny by the courts.

The key principles in the above case were applied by the House of Lords in the following case.

*R (Bancoult) v Secretary of State for Foreign and Commonwealth Affairs
(No 2)* [2009] 1 AC 453

The House of Lords had to decide whether the Crown's prerogative power to legislate by Order in Council on the advice of its ministers in relation to an overseas territory is susceptible to judicial review.

The key principle is that prerogative legislation, made on the advice of ministers, is reviewable by the courts in the same way as prerogative acts. The basis of review is illegality, irrationality, and procedural impropriety.

On the jurisdictional issue the House of Lords decided that the courts had jurisdiction to review the **British Indian Ocean Territory (Constitution) Order 2004** because it was not only part of the local law of the territory but, as imperial legislation, was made in the interests of the undivided realm of the United Kingdom and its non-self-governing territories.

The monarch's Royal Prerogative powers and constitutional conventions

Revision tip

It is important to remember that the way in which the monarch exercises their legal constitutional powers under the Royal Prerogative is governed by significant conventions. This links up with chapter 2 which you may wish to review at this point in your revision to make sure you understand the distinction between law and convention.

The way the monarch exercises their powers is greatly determined by **constitutional conventions**. A monarch must act on the advice of ministers, appoint a member of the House of Commons, who has the confidence of the House, as Prime Minister, appoint government ministers, upon the Prime Minister's recommendation, who are members of either the House of Commons or the House of Lords, normally accept any recommendation made by the Prime Minister to dissolve Parliament, and grant the Royal Assent to every Bill passed by Parliament.

✅ Looking for extra marks?

There is a lot of debate as to whether the monarch has 'personal powers' or 'reserve powers' under the Royal Prerogative to be used in exceptional cases only. There is even disagreement over the precise words to be used to describe them. Compare the views of R Blackburn in 'Monarchy and the Personal Prerogatives' [2004] PL 546 with those of Rodney Brazier in 'Monarchy and the Personal Prerogatives: A Personal Response to Professor Blackburn' [2005] PL 45.

The monarch and the organs and functions of government

Figure 5.1 The monarch and the organs and functions of government

The executive	The legislature	The judiciary
• The head of state • Commander in Chief • Appoints Prime Minister	• Summons and opens Parliament • Dissolves Parliament • Grants the Royal Assent	• Head of the judiciary • Formally appoints judges

The powers of the monarch have largely been delegated to the executive, legislative, and judicial organs of government. The monarch cannot exercise their powers as head of state independently but only as part of and in cooperation with the organs of government and the monarch must exercise their powers, as head of state, in a manner which is compatible with the political principle of democracy and fundamental human rights.

The Privy Council and constitutional monarchy

The Privy Council is one of the oldest parts of government. It supports the legal proposition that the United Kingdom is a constitutional monarchy because all the ministers who are appointed to participate in its policy work must be *Members of Parliament* and be part of a democratically elected government. The *ministerial head of the Privy Council is the President of the Privy Council*. The Privy Council Office provides Secretariat services for the Privy Council (that part of Her Majesty's Government which advises on the exercise of prerogative powers and certain functions assigned to the reigning monarch and the Privy Council by Act of Parliament).

The monarch and the executive

The monarch is the head of the executive and Commander in Chief of the armed forces. But the monarch must exercise their executive powers upon the advice and initiative of their ministers.

Walter Bagehot, in his book entitled *The English Constitution*, 2nd edn (1902), described the monarch's rights as the right to be consulted, to encourage, and to warn.

The monarch and the legislature

The monarch is the only person who has the legal power to dissolve and summon Parliament. Under current law a Parliament comes to an end either at the end of the five year period stipulated by the **Parliament Act 1911** at any time by exercise of the Royal

Prerogative by the monarch acting on the advice of the Prime Minister. The act of dissolving Parliament prior to a General Election is called 'Prorogation by the Crown'. The loss of a vote of no confidence in the House of Commons and party leadership contests are circumstances which may raise questions concerning how the monarch might exercise their powers.

Loss of a vote of no confidence

The Prime Minister is not bound to seek dissolution of Parliament merely because he has been defeated by a vote of the House of Commons. The two possible exceptions appear to be the loss of a vote of no confidence and a vote which makes it impossible for the Prime Minister to continue to govern.

Party leadership contests

There is no need for Parliament to be dissolved if the Prime Minister loses his or her position as leader of the party in power. He or she merely offers their resignation to the monarch who accepts it and offers the post of Prime Minister to the new leader.

Hung parliaments

In *Constitutional Practice*, 3rd edn (1999) ch 3 Rodney Brazier says that the monarch's legal power to appoint a Prime Minister must be used to enhance the democratic process rather than to pre-empt it. So far as possible, the monarch must keep out of the process of government formation. Where there is a hung parliament, the monarch should stand back and let elected politicians decide the shape of the government. If the politicians fail to produce a way forward in a hung parliament the monarch might receive each of the party leaders in turn. Brazier concludes that if a majority coalition government is proposed, rather than the more usual outcome in a hung parliament of a minority government taking office, then such a coalition should be appointed only if the party leaders can work out the details and present a copper-bottomed agreement to the monarch.

The Royal Assent

Could the monarch legitimately refuse the Royal Assent on the ground that, following the **Human Rights Act 1998**, they cannot be compelled to do anything as head of state which violates their right to freedom of speech, conscience, or religion? Robert Blackburn in 'The Royal Assent to Legislation and a Monarch's Fundamental Human Rights' [2003] PL 205 suggests two possible answers. The first, according to Blackburn, is opened up by the **Human Rights Act** itself and relies on the **Regency Acts 1937–1953**. The second focuses on the meaning of 'Royal Assent'. The monarch could either declare that they are not available for the performance of their duties as head of state, due to fundamental human rights grounds of conscience, so that a regent could be temporarily appointed for the purpose of granting the Royal Assent; or define 'Royal Assent' as a narrow duty to certify that a Bill has passed through all its necessary parliamentary stages.

Both here, and in a later article entitled 'Monarchy and the Personal Prerogatives' [2004] PL 546, Blackburn favours the second answer and concludes that the Royal Assent is like a certificate that the bill has passed through all its necessary parliamentary stages; and the monarch cannot refuse the Royal Assent on the grounds of personal views or beliefs.

Rodney Brazier in *Constitutional Practice* offers the following guiding principles. The monarch's legal right to refuse the Royal Assent still exists but must be exercised in a way which is compatible with the political principle of democracy. The modern constitution ought to require political decisions and responsibility for them, to be taken by politicians, and (where appropriate) the electorate, not by the head of state. If a bill seeks to subvert the democratic basis of the constitution the monarch should either grant the Royal Assent under vigorous private protest or insist on a dissolution of Parliament and a General Election.

The monarch and the judiciary

Although, in legal theory, the monarch is the ultimate source of justice, all the monarch's judicial powers are irrevocably delegated to judges and magistrates. The monarch cannot, in person, take part in any legal proceedings, influence the decision of a court, or cause anyone to be arrested for any crime. This was determined by Coke CJ in *Prohibitions del Roy* (1607).

Although judges of the superior courts are, in principle, appointed by the monarch they cannot be dismissed without the consent of both Houses of Parliament. The decisions of inferior courts are subject to reversal on appeal or by judicial review.

The right to appeal to the King or Queen in Council given to UK overseas territories and Crown dependencies has long been delegated to the Judicial Committee of the Privy Council. Today the Judicial Committee of the Privy Council exercises this jurisdiction for all those Commonwealth countries which have retained this right as well as for the Channel Islands and the Isle of Man. In the case of republics appeal is made to the Judicial Committee. The Judicial Committee of the Privy Council consists of the Supreme Court Justices and some senior Commonwealth judges.

Other duties

In addition, the monarch signs state papers, gives audiences to the Prime Minister and visiting ministers from the Commonwealth, receives foreign diplomatic representatives, holds ceremonies to confer honours, attends state occasions, and gives formal consent to appointments.

 Key cases

Case	Facts	Principle
Council of Civil Service Unions v Minister for the Civil Service [1985] AC 374	The Civil Service Union challenged a decision to ban trade union membership at GCHQ on national security grounds.	Although this case was mainly concerned with the justiciability of Royal Prerogative powers delegated to the executive, Lord Roskill (*obiter*) said that powers to dissolve Parliament, appoint ministers, and grant honours 'as well as others' were not justiciable.
M v Home Office [1993] 3 WLR 433	Among other things, the House of Lords had to decide whether the High Court had the power to issue an injunction against the Crown, and, if so was the Home Secretary, in either his personal or ministerial capacity, in contempt of court for ignoring it.	This case draws attention to the fact the term 'the Crown' is capable of having two meanings, namely, the monarch and the executive, to which the monarch's powers have been delegated.
Prohibitions del Roy (1607) 77 ER 1342	The Court of King's Bench had to decide whether the monarch had any right to take part in the judicial process.	The monarch cannot take part in any criminal or civil action or influence the decision of any court of justice. The monarch cannot issue a warrant of arrest.

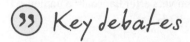 Key debates

Topic	'"Monarchy and the Personal Prerogatives": A Personal Response to Professor Blackburn'
Author/ Academic	Rodney Brazier
Viewpoint	Responds to an earlier article, by Professor Robert Blackburn ([2004] PL 546–563), on the powers of the monarch. Pays particular attention to the monarch's role in appointing a Prime Minister in the event of a hung parliament, the monarch's powers regarding the granting or withholding of Royal Assent, and further issues such as the monarch's role where a Prime Minister acts in breach of convention, and the reserve powers of the monarch.
Source	[2005] PL 45–47.

Exam questions

Topic	'Monarchy and the Personal Prerogatives'
Author/ Academic	Robert Blackburn
Viewpoint	Discusses the role of the monarchy in the conduct and exercise of personal prerogatives. Examines the terminology and thesis of personal prerogatives. Suggests that the theorizing is at odds with political reality. Considers the role and duties of the monarch including the appointment of a Prime Minister, Royal Assent to legislation and the dissolution of Parliament. Assesses the repercussions of talking up of personal prerogatives.
Source	[2004] PL 546–563.

Topic	'The Royal Assent to Legislation and a Monarch's Fundamental Human Rights'
Author/ Academic	Robert Blackburn
Viewpoint	Considers the extent to which the Queen as monarch enjoys fundamental human rights following the enactment of the **Human Rights Act 1998**. Speculates on the possibility of the monarch wishing not to give Royal Assent to a government bill on the ground of moral opposition to it in the light of the right to freedom of thought, conscience and religion in the **Article 9 European Convention on Human Rights 1950**. Suggests how the constitutional problems created by this situation could be resolved either through the appointment of a Regent to give Royal Assent to the bill or by changing the nature of the duty of the head of state to being to simply certify that the bill presented has passed through all required parliamentary and legal processes.
Source	[2003] PL 205–210.

Topic	Judicial review of non-statutory executive powers after Bancoult: a unified anxious model
Author/ Academic	Margit Cohn
Viewpoint	This article studies the review of executive powers in the absence of an empowering statute
Source	[2009] PL 260.

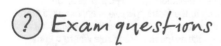 ## ? Exam questions

Problem question

Assume that, following the next General Election, the Conservative Party led by David Cameron, loses its majority in the House of Commons. It soon emerges that a new and extreme political party, called the Reform Party, led by Albert Griscall has won the largest number of seats in the House of Commons. The proposed legislative programme of the Reform Party, set out in its election manifesto, includes measures which would repeal the **Human Rights Act 1998**, the **European Communities Act 1972**, and the **Freedom of Information Act 2000**. Albert Griscall also wishes to enact measures which would allow racial and sex discrimination as well as martial law to deal with anti-social behaviour.

Your advice is sought by the Queen's Private Secretary, who is keen to avert a profound constitutional crisis.

- Advise the Queen's Private Secretary as to the legal and political rules determining who shall be appointed Prime Minister following a General Election and particularly as to whether and upon what basis the Queen might not have to appoint Albert Griscall as Prime Minister.

- Advise the Queen's Private Secretary as to whether, assuming Albert Griscall is appointed to be Prime Minister, the Queen might legitimately refuse to grant the Royal Assent to bills which expressly repeal constitutional statutes.

Outline answers are included at the end of the book.

Essay question

Explain what is meant by Royal Prerogative and the extent to which it is susceptible to legal scrutiny.

Scan here

Scan this QR code image with your mobile device to see an outline answer to this question or log onto www.oxfordtextbooks.co.uk/orc/concentrate

#6

The executive: central, devolved, and local government

Key Facts

- The monarch is the formal head of the executive and the Prime Minister, who is also First Lord of the Treasury and Minister for the Civil Service, advises the monarch on the exercise of all executive powers.

- The Cabinet deals with all matters concerning the collective responsibility of the Government as well as the formulation of government policy and putting it into effect via the parliamentary legislative process.

- Central government in the United Kingdom is organized into departments of state led by Secretaries of State and other ministers whose work is coordinated by the Cabinet.

- Every Secretary of State and minister, including the Prime Minister, is responsible to Parliament and subject to the jurisdiction of the courts.

- The Welsh Assembly Government, the Scottish Government, and the Northern Ireland Executive exercise devolved executive powers within the United Kingdom.

- The executive includes the police and armed forces and Parliament, through legislation, grants executive powers to local authorities.

Revision tip

Make sure you are aware of the meaning of basic legal terms before you revise this topic in detail.

The executive

The executive consists of the reigning monarch who is legally the head of state, the Prime Minister, Cabinet, Secretaries of State, ministers of the Crown, Departments of State, non-departmental public bodies, devolved administrative organizations, local authorities, the police, and the armed forces.

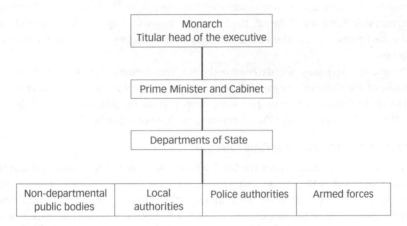

Figure 6.1 The UK executive

Revision tip

This topic links up with the separation of powers covered in chapter 4. It is also provides a foundation for your understanding of judicial review covered in chapters 10 to 12.

The Prime Minister

Revision tip

When you revise this topic you must remember the significant relationship between law and convention within the British Constitution. This topic links with chapters 2 and 4.

Appointment

The Prime Minister is appointed by the reigning monarch. The monarch's powers are governed by binding constitutional conventions. The outgoing Prime Minister offers his resignation to the monarch who accepts it. His or her successor is summoned to the monarch's presence and asked to form a new government.

Following a General Election, this takes place as soon as possible after the result is known, or if there is a hung parliament within a reasonable time if a coalition agreement has to be negotiated. Parliament may object to unreasonable delay.

Powers and duties

The Prime Minister's powers come from the Royal Prerogative and statute. The Prime Minister may advise the monarch on the exercise of all prerogative powers concerning the Government, the appointment of senior members of the judiciary, heads of the intelligence and security services, and senior officers of the Church of England. In conjunction with the Secretary of State for Defence, the Prime Minister is responsible for senior appointments in the armed forces. The Prime Minister makes recommendations for honours and life peerages.

The Prime Minister may also determine the size and membership of the Cabinet, control the agenda of the Cabinet, create and disband Cabinet Committees, and exercise general control over the Cabinet Office by receiving reports from the Secretary of the Cabinet, the Deputy Prime Minister, and the First Secretary of State or other bodies.

The Prime Minister and the Civil Service

The Prime Minister is Minister for the Civil Service. **Section 3** of the **Constitutional Reform and Governance Act 2010** provides that the Minister for the Civil Service has the power to manage the civil service. This includes, among other things, the power to make appointments. The agreement of the Minister for the Civil Service is required in matters concerning the remuneration of civil servants (including compensation payable upon leaving the civil service) or the conditions on which civil servants may retire. In exercising his power to manage the civil service, the Minister for the Civil Service shall have regard to the need to ensure that civil servants who advise ministers are aware of the constitutional significance of Parliament and of the conventions governing the relationship between Parliament and Her Majesty's Government.

The Prime Minister's Office

The Prime Minister has an office with a principal private secretary and private secretaries, a diary secretary, a secretary for appointments, a political secretary, parliamentary private secretaries, press secretaries, and a parliamentary clerk. He also has a Policy Unit, and an Adviser on Efficiency and Effectiveness.

Death or resignation

The death, resignation, or dismissal of the Prime Minister does not automatically lead to a General Election or a change of government or the resignation of the other members of the Cabinet. Any changes in Cabinet membership may be made by the Prime Minister's successor.

Revision tip

Again, remember the constitutional conventions discussed in chapter 2. They have an important role to play in the way the Cabinet works.

The Cabinet

Membership

Members of the Cabinet are chosen by the Prime Minister and appointed by the monarch. The Cabinet may vary in size. In April 2011 the Cabinet consisted of 23 members including one minister without portfolio who does not work within any Department of State.

Functions

The Cabinet deals with questions which concern the **collective responsibility** of the Government because they raise major issues of policy or because they are of critical importance to the public, and deal with unresolved argument between departments. In addition, the Cabinet determines the policy to be submitted to Parliament, including decisions as to the contents of the Queen's speech and the legislative timetable and, the broad economic policy within which the Chancellor of the Exchequer formulates the budget.

Committees

There are standing and ad hoc Cabinet Committees. Standing Committees are permanent. **Ad hoc committees** are set up and empowered by the Cabinet as and when required to deal with current matters of importance. Cabinet Committees may include members who are not part of the Cabinet itself. Particulars of Cabinet committees have been published periodically since 1992.

The Cabinet in relation to the monarch

The monarch does not attend Cabinet meetings. The Prime Minister does so on the monarch's behalf. Ministerial discussions are communicated to the monarch, who is entitled to be fully informed before being asked to approve and sign any documents which are sent via the Prime Minister.

Unanimity of advice and collective Cabinet responsibility

The advice given to the monarch by the Cabinet ought to be unanimous. The monarch may not inquire into any differences of opinion within the Cabinet or express any political views except to ministers or seek advice elsewhere.

The monarch may listen to the views of others without commenting on them.

Collective Cabinet responsibility

Lord Widgery CJ in *AG v Jonathan Cape* **(1975)** (see chapter 2) said that **collective Cabinet responsibility** meant that any policy decision reached by the Cabinet has to be supported thereafter by all members of the Cabinet whether they approve of it or not, unless they feel compelled to resign.

Revision Tip

This area illustrates how the Royal Prerogative, explained in chapter 5 is delegated to the members of the executive. You should review the relevant parts of chapter 2.

Secretaries of State

A **Secretary of State** has delegated authority from the monarch to act in the name of the Crown. They are normally Cabinet **ministers** and Members of Parliament, to which they are accountable.

Under the **European Communities Act 1972** the First Secretary of State is designated minister for transport, consumer protection, the collection of information, employment, medicinal products, and the European agricultural policy.

Departments of State

These implement policies and advise ministers. They are staffed by politically impartial civil servants funded by Parliament. They often work alongside local authorities, non-departmental public bodies, and other government-sponsored organizations. Some departments are responsible for the whole of the United Kingdom. Others are responsible for England and Wales, Scotland, or Northern Ireland. Many departments are headed by ministers. Others are headed by non-ministerial office holders for whose conduct ministers are accountable to Parliament.

Non-departmental public bodies

These are regional or national public bodies which work independently of ministers. There are executive non-departmental public bodies and advisory non-departmental public bodies.

The civil service

Part 1 of the **Constitutional Reform and Governance Act 2010** removes the Royal Prerogative from the management of the civil service and gives the Minister for the Civil Service (the Prime Minister) statutory authority to manage the civil service. The only exceptions are security vetting and the management of the parts of the Civil Service of the State (listed in **s 1**) which are not covered by the provisions in Part 1. The Secretary of State for Foreign and Commonwealth Affairs is given a parallel power to manage the diplomatic service. The Act requires that a code of practice should ensure that civil servants carry out their duty with integrity, honesty, objectivity, and impartiality. The responsibility for appointments to the civil service and hearing complaints is given to the Civil Service Commission. All appointments are to be made on merit on the basis of fair and open competition. The fair and open competition requirement does not apply to special advisers. There is also a requirement for a separate code of conduct for special advisers which provides that special advisers may not authorize the expenditure of public funds, exercise any power in relation to the management of any part of the civil service (except in relation to other special advisers), or otherwise exercise any statutory or prerogative power.

The Civil Service Commission

The Civil Service Commission performs the functions of the former Civil Service Commissioners. The First Civil Service Commissioner and the other Civil Service Commissioners are members of the new Civil Service Commission. Transitional arrangements will enable those serving as Civil Service Commissioners automatically to move across to the new commission.

Parliamentary accountability

Revision tip
This topic provides a foundation for judicial review. See chapters 10 to 12.

According to the Crichel Down Principle, formulated by the House of Commons after the *Crichel Down Affair* (1954), ministers are responsible for the actions and conduct of civil servants in their departments. Accountability arises when a civil servant carries out the minister's explicit order or acts in accordance with policy laid down by the minister or makes a mistake or causes a delay.

The minister is *not* responsible where action is taken by a civil servant of which the minister disapproves and of which he has no previous knowledge, except in the sense that the minister is responsible for the fact that something has gone wrong.

Should a minister resign?

Following the Matrix Churchill Trial (1992), the Report of the Inquiry into the Export of Defence Equipment and Dual-Use Goods to Iraq and Other Prosecutions (1995–96) (The Scott Report), and a debate in the House of Commons the Public Service Committee determined that a minister does not have to resign simply because there has been a failing in their department. A minister should resign if they intentionally mislead the House of Commons.

Revision tip
Looking at the principles of individual ministerial responsibility and collective Cabinet responsibility now will help you to understand the role of Select Committees and the Parliamentary Commissioner for Administration (the Ombudsman) discussed in the next chapter. You should also review what you learned about the distinction between law and convention. See chapter 2.

Legal accountability

In *R v Secretary of State for the Home Department, ex p Oladehinde* (**1991**) the House of Lords (per Lord Griffiths) said that when a statute places a duty on a minister it may be exercised by a member of his department for whom he accepts responsibility and for whose conduct he is legally accountable. Moreover Lord Woolf said, in *M v Home Office* (**1993**) that there appears to be no reason in principle why, if a statute places a duty on a specified minister or other official which creates a cause of action, an action cannot be brought for breach of statutory duty claiming damages or for an injunction against the specified minister personally by any person entitled to benefit from the cause of action.

Revision tip

The accountability of the executive to the judiciary links up with the rule of law discussed in chapter 3 as well as the separation of powers discussed in chapter 4. It provides a foundation for what you will study in chapter 12 on judicial review. It is very important not to restrict your revision to the minimum number of topics required by the assessment.

Devolution

Through the process of devolution, executive powers within the United Kingdom have been given to executive organizations in Scotland, Wales, and Northern Ireland.

Scotland

The Scottish Administration, now called the Scottish Government, was set up by **Pt II Scotland Act 1998**. The Scottish Government consists of the First Minister, the Scottish Ministers, and the Scottish Law Officers.

The First Minister is a member of the Scottish Parliament, is nominated by members of the Scottish Parliament, and appointed by the Queen. The Scottish Ministers are members of the Scottish Parliament. They are appointed by the First Minister and approved by the Scottish Parliament. The Scottish Law Officers are The Lord Advocate and the Solicitor General for Scotland. These are appointed, upon the recommendation of the First Minister and with the agreement of the Scottish Parliament, by the Queen. There are also junior Scottish Ministers who are appointed to assist the Scottish Executive. These are members of the Scottish Parliament and are appointed by the First Minister with the approval of the Scottish Parliament. Executive powers were and continue to be transferred to the Scottish Government within the legislative competence of the Scottish Parliament. There are general provisions for this within the **Scotland Act 1998.** Powers are also transferred by Order in Council.

Wales

Public authorities serving Wales are the Secretary of State for Wales, the Welsh Office, the Welsh Language Board, and the Auditor General for Wales.

Sections 52–55 Government of Wales Act 1998 sets up the Welsh Assembly. The Assembly is empowered to elect the Assembly First Secretary. The Assembly First Secretary is empowered to appoint Assembly Secretaries. The Assembly must establish certain committee. Where additional committees are established, they must (unless they exist solely to provide advice) be elected to reflect the party balance in the Assembly. Sub-committees may also be formed. The Assembly must establish certain committees including the Welsh Administration Ombudsman, the Welsh Development Agency, the Development Board for Rural Wales, the Land Authority for Wales, and Housing for Wales.

The Welsh Assembly Government

The **Government of Wales Act 2006** establishes the Welsh Assembly Government as an entity separate from, but accountable to, the Assembly. It deals with the appointment and remuneration of the First Minister and other ministers and deputy ministers; creates the office of Counsel-General to the Welsh Assembly Government and makes provision for appointment to it; and authorizes the appointment of staff (who are civil servants) in support of the Assembly Government. It provides for the exercise of statutory functions by Ministers in their own right (rather than as delegates of the Assembly), and places duties on them in respect of carrying out regulatory impact assessments in connection with Welsh subordinate legislation, and duties in respect of equality of opportunity, sustainable development, and the Welsh Language. Ministers will also be required to engage with stakeholders through consultation mechanisms with business, local government, and the voluntary sector.

Northern Ireland

The head of the executive in Northern Ireland is the Secretary of State for Northern Ireland acting on behalf of the reigning monarch. Executive powers within Northern Ireland are exercised by the Northern Ireland Executive, the members of which are appointed by the Secretary of State. The **Northern Ireland Act 1998** contained provisions concerning the Government of Northern Ireland including the creation of the Northern Ireland Assembly. This was suspended by the **Northern Ireland Act 2000**.

The Northern Ireland institutions, including the Northern Ireland Assembly, were suspended in October 2002. Plans to restore a devolved executive in Northern Ireland were contained in the **Northern Ireland Act 2006**. Government proposals, incorporated in this Act, involved bringing together Assembly members to participate in a process to select a Northern Ireland Executive, comprising a First Minister, a deputy First Minister and Northern Ireland Ministers. At the time of writing the Northern Ireland Assembly is now up and running.

London: the Mayor and the Greater London Authority

Section 1 Greater London Authority Act 1999 creates the Greater London Authority. **Section 2** says that the Greater London Authority shall consist of the Mayor of London and an Assembly for London called the London Assembly.

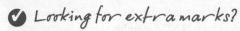 **Looking for extra marks?**

You should now go to the key debates section of this guide and read the recommended articles. There is a lot of material on devolution issues in Scotland, Wales, and Northern Ireland to be found online. You should follow this up.

Local government

England

England consists of the combined areas of the counties, districts, and unitary authorities created by the **Local Government Act 1972**, as amended by the **Local Government Act 1985** and the **Local Government Act 1992**, together with the combined areas of Greater London and the Metropolitan Police District, formed by the **London Government Act 1963**, the **Local Government Act 1985** and the **Police Act 1996**, and the **Greater London Authority Act 1999**. Under **s 2(1) London Government Act 1963** the administrative area of Greater London means the combined areas of the London boroughs, the City of London, the Inner Temple, and the Middle Temple. Under the **Police Act 1996**, as amended and supplemented by the **Greater London Authority Act 1999**, the Metropolitan Police District, means Greater London, excluding the City of London and the Inner Temple and the Middle Temple.

Looking for extra marks?

Attempts to extend devolution to the English regions have been less successful than in Scotland, Wales, and Northern Ireland. There has also been some opposition to proposed local government reforms in England. You should follow this up in your recommended standard textbook and look up the journal articles available online and think about the future of England within a devolved United Kingdom.

Wales

Following the **Local Government (Wales) Act 1994** Wales consists of twenty-two Unitary Authorities.

Scotland

Following the **Local Government (Scotland) Act 1994**, Scotland is the combined areas of 29 unitary authorities and three island authorities. Under the **Island of Rockall Act 1972** as amended by the **Local Government (Scotland) Act 1973 s 214(2), Sch 27, Pt II, para 202**, the Island of Rockall is part of Scotland.

Northern Ireland

Section 43(2) Northern Ireland Constitution Act 1973 provides that Northern Ireland consists of the parliamentary counties of Antrim, Armagh, Down, Fermanagh, Londonderry, and Tyrone and the parliamentary boroughs of Belfast and Londonderry.

The Police in England and Wales

The police forces within the UK are part of the executive. The organization of the police in England and Wales is contained in the **Police Act 1996** and the **Police Reform Act 2002**. **Part 1 and Sch 1 Police Act 1996** contain provisions for the organisation of police forces and police areas in England and Wales. England and Wales is divided up into police areas.

A police force is maintained within each police area. A 'Police Authority' is established to secure the maintenance of an efficient and effective police force for its area. Police Authorities must determine policing objectives on an annual basis and issue a plan setting out the proposed arrangements for the policing of the authority's area during the year. Each Police Authority must keep a fund known as the police fund. Police forces are organized under the direction of a chief constable appointed by the Police Authority, subject to approval by the Secretary of State. There is also an assistant chief constable.

The other ranks, which may be held in a police force, are superintendent, chief inspector, inspector, sergeant, and constable. The creation of additional ranks, as well as changes to existing ranks, may be made by Regulation. A Police Authority may employ civilians to assist the police force maintained by it to enable the authority to discharge its functions. In addition, a Police Authority may appoint a 'clerk to the authority'. Police Authorities may appoint or designate a person, who is not employed by it, under s 17 of the **1996 Act**.

Under the **Police Act 1996** London is composed of the Metropolitan Police District and the City of London Police Area. Under **s 101(1) Police Act 1996** 'Metropolitan Police District' means that district as defined in **s 76 London Government Act 1963**. This is modified by the **Greater London Authority Act 1999**. **Section 101(1) Police Act 1996** provides that 'chief officer of police' means, in relation to the Metropolitan Police force, the Commissioner of Police of the Metropolis. The Police Authority for the Metropolitan Police District is the Home Secretary. The expenses of the Metropolitan Police are met out of the Metropolitan Police Fund.

Section 56 City of London Police Act 1839 empowers the Common Council of the City of London to set up a police committee for the purpose of exercising such powers in connection with the police as the Common Council delegates to it. **Section 101(1) Police Act 1996** provides that in relation to the City of London Police Force, the chief officer of police means the Commissioner of Police of the City of London. The expenses of the City of London Police Force are met out of the City of London Police Fund.

Key cases

Case	Facts	Principle
Carltona v Commissioners of Works [1943] 2 All ER 560	The Court of Appeal had to decide whether a minister could be legally accountable for mistakes made by civil servants employed in his department.	Ministers have legal responsibility for whatever happens in their departments. It is the minister who is sued, not the civil servant. The courts accept and recognize the convention that a civil servant often acts in the name of ministers.
M v Home Office [1991] 3 All ER 537	The House of Lords had to decide whether the Home Secretary was subject to the compulsory jurisdiction of the court.	There appears to be no reason in principle why, if a statute places a duty on a specified minister or other official which creates a cause of action, an action cannot be brought for breach of statutory duty claiming damages or for an injunction, an action cannot be brought for breach of statutory duty claiming damages or for an injunction, against the specified minister personally by any person entitled to benefit from the cause of action.
R v Secretary of state for the Home Department, ex p Oladehinde [1991] 1 AC 254	The House of Lords had to decide whether the Home Secretary was legally responsible for the conduct of immigration officers.	When a statute places a duty on a minister it may generally be exercised by a member of his department for whom he accepts responsibility and for whose conduct he is accountable.
R v Skinner [1968] 2 QB 700	The question to be considered by the Court was whether the minister could delegate a decision to use breathalysing equipment.	Ministers are not expected to take every decision entrusted to them by Parliament. If a decision is made on his behalf by one of his officials, then that is the minister's constitutional decision.

🗩 Key debates

Topic	'The Significance of Parliamentary Procedures in Control of the Executive: A Case Study: The Passage of Part 1 of the Legislative and Regulatory Reform Act 2006'
Author/Academic	Peter Davis
Viewpoint	Discusses the provisions of the **Pt 1 Legislative and Regulatory Reform Act 2006** in terms of its effect on the role of parliamentary procedures in controlling the executive.
Source	[2007] PL 677–700.

Topic	'A Brown Constitution'
Author/Academic	Neil Parpworth
Viewpoint	Discusses some of the constitutional reform proposals put forward by Prime Minister Gordon Brown in a speech to Parliament on 3 July 2007, including the ending of the Prime Minister's prerogative power to request the dissolution of Parliament.
Source	[2007] L Ex (Aug) 14–16.

Topic	'Governing Devolution: Understanding the Office of First Ministers in Scotland and Wales'
Author/Academic	Peter Lynch
Viewpoint	Assesses, using academic material on Prime Ministerial power, the role and functions of First Ministers in Scotland and Wales in comparison with those of the UK Prime Minister. Discusses the power and resources available to each First Minister, the extent to which they have freedom to intervene in policymaking, their power to hire and fire ministers at all levels and considers whether First Ministers are both party leaders as well as heads of government.
Source	(2006) 59(3) Parliamentary Affairs 420–436.

Topic	'The Dawn of Devolution'
Author/Academic	Seamus Burns
Viewpoint	Comments on the deal between the Democratic Unionist Party and Sinn Fein to establish a cross-community, power sharing executive in Northern Ireland from 8 May 2007, and discusses its background, including the democratic mandate, talks and negotiations, and the end of direct rule with the restarting of devolution on 26 March 2007.
Source	(2007) 157(7271) NLJ, 613–614.

Topic	'Power to the Welsh'
Author/Academic	Bridgette Wilcox
Viewpoint	Discusses the provisions of the **Government of Wales Act 2006**, which separates the executive and legislature. Argues that English lawyers need to be aware of the differences between English and Welsh law.
Source	(2007) 21(15) Lawyer 25.

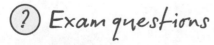

(?) Exam questions

Problem question

Assume that the Government introduces a bill into Parliament to make all universities private companies. All the members of the Cabinet support the bill except the Home Secretary. He has

Exam questions

✱✱✱✱✱✱✱✱✱✱

spoken out against the bill on television and in Parliament. The Prime Minister also discovers that, owing to a mistake made by civil servants at the Home Office the cost of introducing identity cards is 500% more than reported to the House of Commons. There are calls for the Home Secretary's resignation.

Advise the Home Secretary as to:

- whether he is obliged to resign; and,
- his parliamentary and legal responsibility, if any, for the errors made by the team of civil servants at the Home Office.

Outline answers are included at the end of the book.

Essay question

Explain the principle of devolution and the extent to which executive powers have been devolved equally throughout the United Kingdom.

 Scan here

Scan this QR code image with your mobile device to see an outline answer to this question or log onto www.oxfordtextbooks.co.uk/orc/concentrate

#7

Parliament

Key Facts

- The UK legislature is the Monarch in Parliament.

- The UK Parliament is bicameral, with two chambers namely the House of Commons and the House of Lords.

- The House of Lords, which is composed of life peers, senior bishops, and some hereditary peers, protects the constitution, and initiates and revises legislation.

- The House of Commons, which is composed of constituency representatives organized on party lines under the whip system, is the principal legislative chamber and plays a significant role in scrutinizing the executive.

- Both the House of Commons and the House of Lords are representative chambers but only the House of Commons is composed of elected representatives.

- Members of the House of Commons are elected according to the 'first past the post' electoral system.

- There are alternative electoral systems, based on proportional representation, some of which are used within the United Kingdom.

- Part of the legislative function, within the United Kingdom, has been devolved to the Scottish Parliament, the National Assembly for Wales, and the Northern Ireland Assembly.

The United Kingdom legislature

The legislature of the United Kingdom is the Queen in Parliament. Parliament is bicameral. This means that, apart from the Queen, there are two legislative chambers called the House of Lords and the House of Commons. They work separately and simultaneously.

The House of Lords

Under the **House of Lords Act 1999** the House of Lords consists of life peers, senior bishops of the Church of England, and hereditary peers.

Disclaimer and disqualification

Under the **Peerage Act 1963** hereditary peers may disclaim their titles for life and thus become eligible for membership of the House of Commons. Aliens, bankrupts, persons under the age of 21, and persons sentenced to imprisonment for treason may not sit in the House of Lords.

The functions and business of the House of Lords

The House of Lords is the 'Protector of the Constitution'. The Lords have the power to reject a bill seeking to extend the life of a parliament beyond five years. The House of Lords is also the place where many private and public bills are introduced into Parliament. The most important function of the House of Lords is the revision and scrutiny of bills.

The House of Lords scrutinizes the executive through debates and select committees.

The Salisbury Doctrine

The House of Lords shall not, at its second or third reading, reject a government bill which has come from the House of Commons based on an electoral mandate from the nation. An electoral mandate from the nation means something contained in a General Election manifesto. This is the Salisbury Doctrine or Salisbury Convention.

The House of Commons

Minors, aliens, peers, clerics, psychiatric patients, bankrupts, persons convicted of corrupt or illegal practices, prisoners, excess ministers, members of other legislatures, holders of public office, and holders of offices for profit under the Crown may not sit in the House of Commons.

Expulsion

The House may declare a disqualified member's seat vacant or may expel a member for whatever reason it pleases.

The principal functions of the House of Commons

The House of Commons exclusively initiates financial legislation. It sustains, checks, and balances the power of the government. It also represents the interests and grievances of constituents and promotes the interests of the nation in times of emergency. The House of Commons makes a leading contribution to the overall effectiveness of Parliament.

The House of Commons uses Question Time, debates, and Select Committees to carry out its functions.

Question Time

This occupies between 50 and 60 minutes and includes Prime Minister's Question Time. There are questions requiring oral answers, those requiring written answers, and private notice questions.

Debates

The House of Commons scrutinizes government policy in the second reading stage of a bill, substantive motions for debate moved by the Government, substantive motions for debate moved by the opposition, the address in reply to the Queen's Speech, and the debate following budget proposals.

Select Committees

These are smaller than **standing committees**. The select committee usually comprises up to 15 MPs with the various parties being represented according to their proportion of seats in the House. The types of select committee include the following:

Ad hoc Committees

These committees are set up to look into and report on specific matters. Today much of the work which used to be done by such committees is now done by **Royal Commissions**, **Tribunals of Inquiry**, departmental committees, and committees of inquiry chaired by senior members of the judiciary.

Permanent Select Committees

The Permanent, or regular, Select Committees of the House of Commons include the **Public Accounts Committee,** the Select Committee on European Legislation, the Select Committee on the Parliamentary Commissioner, the Select Committee of Privileges (now Standards and Privileges), and the Select Committees on services, selection and procedure.

Departmental Select Committees

Government departments are scrutinized by select committees. The number of such committees depends on the number of government departments in existence at any given time.

The Parliamentary Commissioner for Administration

The Parliamentary Commissioner for Administration (the Ombudsman) was set up by the **Parliamentary Commissioner Act 1967**. This Act was subsequently amended by the **Parliamentary and Health Service Commissioners Act 1987** and the **Parliamentary Commissioner Act 1994**.

Purpose and jurisdiction

The purpose of the Ombudsman is to receive and deal with complaints from individuals who have suffered injustice because of maladministration. There is no statutory definition of maladministration. In 1966, Richard Crossman said that it includes bias, neglect, inattention, delay, incompetence, ineptitude, perversity, turpitude, and arbitrariness. Subsequently, this has been expanded to take into account categories of discrimination. The Ombudsman's jurisdiction is limited by **ss 5** and **6** and **Schs 2** and **3 Parliamentary Commissioner Act 1967**. There are detailed lists of excluded matters and bodies.

Procedure

According to **s 5** of the **1967 Act**, anyone who wishes to make a complaint has to go through an MP. In practice, if a complaint is made directly to the Ombudsman by a member of the public it is referred to an MP who, at their discretion, refers it back to the Ombudsman. If the complaint is accepted, the Ombudsman conducts a private enquiry according to the terms of **s 7** of the **1967 Act**. The end result of the investigation is a report which is considered by the Select Committee on Public Administration.

Where the Ombudsman finds maladministration remedial action can be recommended. Remedial action consists of payment of compensation, alterations of decisions or procedures, and giving an apology.

The Ombudsman has no power to require compliance with any recommendations.

✔ *Looking for extra marks?*

There have been a number of proposals for reform in this area and there are several useful publications available online at www.cabinetoffice.gov.uk. You should look up these publications and think about how the ombudsman service could be improved.

Electoral law

Revision tip

This topic is closely linked with the principle of democracy. This is a political principle and not easy to define. To avoid confusion, when you revise this part of the topic, stick to the key rules which apply to British constitutional law. Focus now on the legal right to vote in an election and what is meant by 'free elections'.

The right to vote in an election

At common law anyone qualified to vote in an election has the right to do so and may bring a claim for damages in tort against any person who illegally excludes him.

....

Ashby v White (1703) 92 ER 126; (1703) 92 ER 710; 1 ER 417

This was determined by the House of Lords, which overruled the decision of the Court of Queen's Bench and followed the dissenting judgment of Holt CJ from which the following key principles emerge. If a statute gives a right the common law will provide a remedy to maintain it where there is injury or damage. The court's jurisdiction to provide remedies for breaches of legal rights is not limited by parliamentary privilege.

....

Free elections

The principle of **free elections** was enacted by **Article 8 Bill of Rights 1689**, which provides that the parliamentary elections ought to be free. Moreover, **Article 3 European Convention on Human Rights and Fundamental Freedoms (1953) First Protocol** provides that the High Contracting Parties undertake to hold free elections at reasonable intervals by secret ballot, under conditions which will ensure the free expression of the opinion of the people in the choice of the legislature. This was incorporated into UK law by the **Human Rights Act 1998**.

Revision tip

One of the important things to be clear about at this stage is that although democracy implies government by the people, in British constitutional law, the word 'people' does not mean the general population. You need to understand the nature and extent of the franchise, the electorate, and the organization of constituencies.

The franchise and the electorate

The franchise is the legal right to vote. The electorate is all those who have this right. The rules are found in the **Representation of the People Act 1983** as amended by the **Representation of the People Act 2000**. To qualify an elector must be 18 years of age or over at the time of the election, be a British subject, or citizen of the Republic of Ireland (any EU national resident in the United Kingdom may vote in elections for the European Parliament), and not be subject to any legal disqualification.

The **Representation of the People Act 1989** allows UK citizens who live abroad to vote if they have been resident in the United Kingdom and registered as voters within the previous 20 years. Service personnel are entitled to be considered 'resident' providing that their absence results from service for the armed forces or the Crown overseas. Similar provisions apply to merchant seamen.

The **Representation of the People Act 2000** creates the concept of 'rolling' electoral registration. Thus an electoral register for any given constituency will be produced for a specific election based on an annual return as amended by any subsequent changes.

Section 3 of the **2000 Act** deals with the residence requirements considered by registration officers when deciding whether or not to register a person as a voter. Regard will be had to the purpose of the residence and other circumstances. **Section 7** enables service voters to register on this basis provided the criteria under **s 3** are met. A person whose name is not on the register may not vote. It is a criminal offence to vote in more than one constituency (other than as a proxy for another elector). Even if a person's name is on the register, it is a criminal offence to vote if ineligible to do so. Those disqualified from voting include aliens, minors, mental defectives and drunkards. Under the **2000 Act** a person who is detained in a mental hospital as a voluntary patient may be registered as a voter provided his stay is sufficient in length for him to be regarded as resident in the mental hospital. Most convicted criminals serving sentences of imprisonment as well as persons convicted of corrupt or illegal practices at elections are disqualified from voting.

Constituencies

The delimitation of constituencies is a matter for Parliament. Prior to the enactment of the **Political Parties, Elections and Referendums Act 2000,** the determination of constituency boundaries was undertaken by four Boundary Commissions for England, Wales, Scotland, and Northern Ireland. Under the **Political Parties, Elections and Referendums Act 2000**, that task is transferred to the Electoral Commission.

The redistribution of seats is a controversial matter as political parties can lose 'safe' seats because of it. Although there have been a number of challenges in the courts to decisions of the Boundary Commissioners, none have succeeded.

....

R v Boundary Commission for England, ex p Foot [1983] QB 600

The Court of Appeal had to decide whether it had jurisdiction to decide if a decision of the Boundary Commission could be challenged on the ground that it had acted unreasonably. The Court of Appeal held that although there was no statutory right of appeal against a decision of the Boundary Commission, the High Court had jurisdiction to determine whether the Boundary Commission had properly carried out its statutory instructions. The rules followed by the Boundary Commission were guidelines only. The substantial obstacle to judicial review of the Boundary Commission was that it did not make decisions but recommendations for which it did not have to give reasons. The claimant would have to prove that the Boundary Commission's recommendations and conclusions were such that no reasonable commission could have made them. The claimants had failed to discharge their burden of proof in this case. Their claim for judicial review failed.

. . . .

The Parliamentary Voting System and Constituencies Act 2011

Sections **10 to 14** update and set out the current powers of the Boundary Commission. **Section 11** of the Act provides that there shall be 600 constituencies within the United Kingdom of not more than 13,000 square kilometres unless it is at least 12,000 square kilometres and the Boundary Commission concerned is satisfied that it is not reasonably possible for the constituency to comply with that rule. The Act goes on to make further provisions for determining constituency boundaries.

Conduct of electoral campaigns: voting systems

The responsibility for the conduct of elections lies with the returning officer who is the Sheriff of the County or Mayor of the Borough, depending on the constituency. Their authority is delegated to the registration officer for each constituency. Voting is by way of secret ballot. The candidate who receives the highest number of votes in each constituency is 'returned' as the Member of Parliament for that constituency. There is no requirement that a candidate must obtain a minimum percentage of the total vote to be elected. This system of voting is known as the 'first past the post' system.

Alternative voting systems

Revision tip

While there may be agreement that a legislature should be representative and composed of elected members there are many different views about the best way to achieve a genuinely representative legislature. You may be asked, in an essay question in particular, to compare, contrast, and assess the various alternative systems. Again, to avoid confusion, you should emphasize their legal and procedural effectiveness. You are concerned purely with the legal technicalities.

Single member systems

The supplementary vote

With the supplementary vote, there are two columns on the ballot paper – one for the first choice and one for the second choice. Voters are not required to make a second choice if they do not wish to. Voters mark an 'X' in the first column for their first choice and a second 'X' in the second column for their other choice. Voters' first preferences are counted and if one candidate gets 50% of the vote, then he or she is elected. If no candidate reaches 50% of the vote, the two highest scoring candidates are retained and the rest of the candidates are eliminated. The second preferences on the ballot papers of the eliminated candidates are examined and any that have been cast for the two remaining candidates are given to them. Whoever has the most votes at the end of the process wins.

The system is used to elect the Mayor of London.

Multi-member systems

Single transferable vote (STV)

Each constituency would elect between three and five MPs depending on its size. Voters rank the candidates, putting a '1' for their favourite, a '2' for the next, and so on. If the voter's first choice candidate does not need their vote, either because he or she is elected without it, or because he or she has too few votes to be elected, then the vote is transferred to the voter's second choice candidate, and so on.

In this way, most of the votes help to elect a candidate and far fewer votes are wasted. An important feature of **STV** is that voters can choose between candidates both of their own and of other parties, and can even select candidates for reasons other than party affiliation. Thus, a voter, wishing for more women MPs could vote for a woman from their own party and then all other women candidates, whatever party they stand for.

The system is used: in the Australian Senate, the Republic of Ireland, Tasmania, Malta, and Northern Ireland for local elections and elections to the European Parliament.

Arguments used in favour

STV does more than other systems to guarantee that everyone gets their views represented in Parliament and that they have a say in what is done by their elected representatives. STV is the best option for putting the power in the hands of the voters and keeping MPs linked to the people who voted for them. Most voters can identify a representative that they personally helped to elect and can feel affinity with. Such a personal link also increases accountability.

Making Parliament reflect the views of the voters

Only a party or coalition of parties, who could attract more than 50% of the electorate, could form a government. Any changes would have to be backed by a majority since public opinion is reflected fairly in elections under STV. This is far more important than that a government should be formed by only one political party.

It enables the voters to express opinions effectively. Voters can choose between candidates within parties, demonstrating support for different wings of the party. Voters can also express preferences between the abilities or other attributes, of individual candidates.

It is simple for voters to use

There is no need for tactical voting. Voters can cast a positive vote and know that their vote will not be wasted whatever their choice is. It produces governments that are strong and stable because they are founded on the majority support of the electorate.

Weaknesses

The system does not produce such accuracy in proportional representation of parties as the party list or additional member systems. It breaks the link between *an individual* MP and his or her constituency. Constituencies would be three to five times larger than they are now but with three to five MPs. MPs may have to spend an excessive amount of time dealing with constituency problems and neglect the broader issues. There are critics who say that this system could lead to permanent coalition governments, but this would only happen if the voters as a whole want it. It is disliked by politicians, since it would remove power from them and give it to the electors, and many MPs with safe seats would lose the security they feel now.

Mixed systems
Additional member system (AMS)

Several variants of Additional Member Systems have been proposed, but basically they are a combination of the 'first past the post' system and party list voting. The purpose is to retain the best features of 'first past the post' while introducing proportionality between parties through party list voting.

Each voter has two votes, one vote for a single MP via 'first past the post', and one for a regional or national party list. Half the seats or more are allocated to the single-member constituencies and the rest to the party list. The percentage of votes obtained by the parties in the party list vote determines their overall number of representatives; the party lists are used to top up the 'first past the post' seats gained by the party to the required number. So if a party has won two seats in the constituencies but in proportion to its votes should have five, the first three candidates on its list are elected in addition.

The system is used in Germany and it was also chosen by New Zealand in a referendum in 1993, (although in New Zealand it is called Mixed Member Proportional Representation or MMP). The new Scottish Parliament and the Welsh Assembly were both elected by AMS in May 1999 and 2003 as was the London Assembly in May 2000.

Arguments used in favour

It results in broadly proportional representation along party lines while ensuring that there is a directly accountable MP for each constituency. It retains a number of single-member constituencies. It has produced strong and stable governments in Germany (but not single party governments). Each elector has at least one effective vote. Even if they see no chance of winning in the single-member constituency, people can use their second vote for a party they support and still have a limited say through an additional member. The separation of the vote allows the voter to make an expression of popular approval or disapproval which is not possible under 'first past the post'. Because the first vote does not affect a party's total representation, a voter can use it to express personal support for a candidate without necessarily helping that candidate's party. AMS would give people the government they wanted, keeping the link between MPs and voters as well as giving some value to all votes, via the additional members.

Weaknesses

It combines many of the faults of 'first past the post' with many of the defects of the list systems of PR. Half of all MPs are not directly accountable to any voters, just to their party leadership, and have no constituency. It creates two types of MP, one with a constituency role and duties and one without such a base. To retain some constituency MPs, constituencies would have to increase in size. The parties would retain power over selecting candidates for constituency seats and would have complete control over choosing their Additional Members. Those who are under-represented today may not fare any better under AMS.

The Independent Commission on the Voting System (The Jenkins Report) made a number of significant recommendations, the most important of which was that the best alternative for Britain to the 'first past the post' system is a two-vote mixed system which can be described as either limited AMS or AV top-up.

The **Parliamentary Voting System and Constituencies Act 2011** provided for a referendum to determine whether the first past the post system ought to be replaced by AV. The referendum was held on 5 May 2011. The result favoured the retention of the first past the post system for General Elections.

Revision tip

Important legislative functions have been delegated under the principle of devolution. You should study this closely.

The devolution of the legislative function

Scotland

The Scottish Parliament is set up by **s 1 Scotland Act 1998**.

The Scottish Parliament can legislate generally subject to the restrictions in **ss 28** and **29** and **Sch 4 Scotland Act 1998**. Acts of the Scottish Parliament are subordinate legislation because they owe their validity to the **Scotland Act 1998**. They can be set aside by the courts and overridden by Acts of the UK Parliament. According to **s 28** the validity of the procedure leading to an enactment does not affect the Act's validity. But Acts of the Scottish Parliament that are outside its competence are not law. Where a measure is ambiguous it must be interpreted narrowly in favour of its validity according to **s 101 Scotland Act 1998**.

Restrictions

The Scottish Parliament cannot, except in minor respects, amend the **Scotland Act 1998**. It cannot alter law outside Scotland. It cannot override European Union law, or rights binding under the **Human Rights Act 1998**. UK ministers have the exclusive powers to bring EU law into effect. It has taxation powers limited to altering the basic rate of income tax by three pence in the pound.

Reserved matters

Many important matters are reserved matters on which only the UK Parliament can legislate. They include important constitutional provisions including matters affecting the Crown (but not the exercise of the royal prerogative), the civil service, the registration and funding of political parties, the Union with England, the UK Parliament, the higher Scottish courts, international relations, defence, national security, treason, fiscal, economic, and monetary policy, currency, financial services and market, money laundering, border controls, transport safety and regulation, media policy, employment regulation, certain health matters, and the regulation of key professions and social security.

The devolution of legislative competence to the Scottish Parliament does not affect the ability of Westminster to legislate for Scotland even in relation to devolved matters. But, under the so-called Sewel Convention, the Westminster Parliament will not normally legislate with regard to devolved matters in Scotland without the consent of the Scottish Parliament.

Wales

The **Government of Wales Act 1998** establishes a National Assembly for Wales (the Welsh Assembly) consisting of 60 Assembly Members (AMs). Forty AMs were elected on a 'first past the post' basis from constituencies identical with parliamentary constituencies and a further 20 AMs were elected from five electoral regions, four from each region. The Welsh Assembly's powers, whether transferred by Orders in Council or conferred directly by Act of Parliament, include a large number of subordinate order-making powers (including some powers enabling the Assembly to amend primary legislation), but the Assembly was not empowered by the 1998 Act to make primary legislation for Wales.

The **Government of Wales Act 2006** provides that the Welsh Assembly is no longer a corporate body, makes amendments to the electoral law, creates the Welsh Assembly Government, and deals with some issues concerning the powers of the Secretary of State for Wales.

The legislative competence of the Welsh Assembly

The Welsh Assembly was reconstituted as a separate legislature following elections in May 2007. **Section 94** and **Sch 5 Government of Wales Act 2006** gives the Welsh Assembly the power to make laws called Measures of the National Assembly for Wales (Assembly Measures). The legislative competence of the Welsh Assembly is set out in **Sch 5**. An Assembly Measure is within the legislative competence of the Welsh Assembly if it relates to agriculture, fisheries, forestry, rural development, ancient monuments, historic buildings, culture, economic development, education and training. In March 2011 a referendum was held in Wales to determine whether the Welsh Assembly should be given further legislative powers in accordance with the provisions of **Part 4** of the **2006 Act**. 63.5% of people voted yes and 36.5% of people voted no in the referendum. The Welsh Assembly will, in the future, be able to make laws for Wales on subjects for which the Assembly and the Welsh Assembly Government are already responsible, without needing permission from the UK Parliament first.

Revision Tip

The process of legislative devolution has been particularly problematic in Northern Ireland. You should consider the issues carefully.

Northern Ireland

The **Northern Ireland Act 1998** set up the Northern Ireland Assembly. This was suspended by the **Northern Ireland Act 2000**. The Northern Ireland Assembly ceased to function from October 2002. The **Northern Ireland Assembly (Elections and Periods of Suspension) Act 2003** postponed the date of the poll for the election of the next Northern Ireland Assembly from 29 May 2003, set by the **Northern Ireland Assembly Elections Act 2003**, and provided a mechanism for setting the date of the next poll. The **Northern Ireland Act 2006** recalled the Members of the Northern Ireland Assembly to sit in a '2006 Assembly' whose focus was to provide a forum for the parties to begin preparations for devolved government. It set a deadline of 24 November 2006 for the parties to have made sufficient progress to allow for devolution to be fully restored. The next legislative step was the **Northern Ireland (Miscellaneous Provisions) Act 2006.** This Act made provision concerning registration of electors, Chief Electoral Officer for Northern Ireland ('CEO'), donations for political purposes, devolution of policing and justice, extension of the amnesty period for arms decommissioning, loans to the Northern Ireland Consolidated Fund, single wholesale electricity market, financial assistance for energy purposes, sustainable development, extending certain provisions of the Serious Organised Crime and Police Act 2005 ('SOCAP') to Northern Ireland, health and safety of police officers, and duty to fill judicial vacancies.

The **Northern Ireland (St Andrews Agreement) Act 2006** set up a transitional Assembly. A poll was held on 7 March 2007. Following this, a permanent assembly was set up.

✔ *Looking for extra marks?*

You should follow up this subject by reading the articles recommended under key debates in this guide as well as by reading your recommended standard textbook.

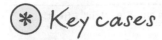 **Key cases**

Case	Facts	Principle
Ashby v White (1704)	The Court of Queen's bench and the House of Lords had to decide whether a person deprived of an opportunity to vote when they had a legal right to do so had a cause of action in tort.	If a statute gives a right the common law will provide a remedy to maintain it where there is injury or damage in spite of parliamentary privilege.
R v Boundary Commission for England ex p Foot [1983] QB 600	The Court of Appeal had to decide whether it had jurisdiction to decide if a decision of the Boundary Commission could be challenged.	The Court of Appeal held that the court would not intervene unless the claimant could prove that the Boundary Commission's recommendations and conclusions were such that no reasonable commission could have made them.

Key debates

Topic	'The Governance of Britain'
Author/Academic	Ministry of Justice: Green Paper
Viewpoint	Among other things, this Green Paper sets out government proposals to reform the functions and procedures of the legislature.
Source	The Stationery Office.

Topic	'Gordon Brown's New Constitutional Settlement'
Author/Academic	Andrew Le Sueur
Viewpoint	Comments on the constitutional reforms proposed in the July 2007 Green Paper entitled *The Governance of Britain*.
Source	[2008] PL 21–27.

Topic	'"The Greatest Quango of Them All", "A Rival Chamber" or "A Hybrid Nonsense"? Solving the Second Chamber Paradox'
Author/Academic	Gavin Phillipson
Viewpoint	Comments on the constitutional challenges facing Government proposals to reform the House of Lords.
Source	[2004] PL 352–379.

Exam questions

✱✱✱✱✱✱✱✱✱✱✱✱

Topic	'British Elections – Additional Members and the "Neill" Effect'
Author/Academic	Oonagh Gay
Viewpoint	Looks at use of additional member system in Scottish, Welsh, and European elections.
Source	[1999] PL 185–199.

Topic	'Westminster as a Three-in-One Legislature for the United Kingdom and its Devolved Territories'
Author/Academic	Robert Hazell
Viewpoint	Discusses the extent to which the Westminster Parliament still operates as a three-in-one legislature, legislating for the whole of the UK.
Source	(2007) 13(2) Journal of Legislative Studies 254–279.

 Exam questions

Essay question 1

Critically assess whether proportional representation or 'first past the post' ought to be adopted in General Elections to the House of Commons.

Essay question 2

Explain the extent to which the legislative powers of the UK Parliament have been permanently delegated to the Scottish Parliament and the Welsh and Northern Ireland Assembly.

 Scan here

Scan this QR code image with your mobile device to see outline answers to these questions or log onto www.oxfordtextbooks.co.uk/orc/concentrate

#8

The legislative process and the sovereignty of parliament

Key Facts

- An Act of Parliament is a bill which has, at common law, received the separate and simultaneous assents of the House of Commons and the House of Lords as well as the Royal Assent.

- Under the **Parliament Acts 1911 and 1949** a bill may become an Act of Parliament by receiving the assent of the House of Commons and the Royal Assent.

- Public bills, which originate largely within government departments, pass between the House of Commons and the House of Lords and undergo detailed scrutiny in committees set up by each House.

- The legislative supremacy of Parliament is a jurisdictional question: Parliament has unlimited power to make and unmake laws and, once the courts have determined that a bill has become an Act of Parliament, they have no jurisdiction to override it or set it aside.

- Cases following the House of Lords' decision in *Pepper v Hart* (1992) suggest that the courts may be willing to exercise their jurisdiction to interpret statutes more generously.

- Although any legislative provision may be expressly repealed by Parliament, the courts have jurisdiction to determine whether an Act of Parliament is a constitutional statute and immune from the common law doctrine of implied repeal.

- The **Human Rights Act 1998** requires the courts to interpret statutes in a way which is consistent with Convention rights and enables the High Court in England and Wales to make declarations of incompatibility.

Parliament and legislation

A bill is a draft statute, introduced into Parliament which, if passed, becomes an Act of Parliament. There are public, private, and hybrid bills.

A public bill seeks to make or change the law affecting people's rights and obligations generally in all or part of the United Kingdom. A private bill aims to confer upon or regulate the rights and obligations of individuals and corporate bodies. A hybrid bill concerns the general law and the rights and obligations of individuals and corporations.

At common law an Act of Parliament is a bill which has received the separate and simultaneous assents of the House of Lords and the House of Commons and the Royal Assent.

....

Stockdale v Hansard (1839) 112 ER 1112

This was determined by Lord Denman CJ. The question was whether the House of Commons could extend its own privileges by resolution.

It was held that the House of Commons cannot make or amend laws by resolution. For this purpose legislation is required which has received the simultaneous and separate assents of the House of Commons and the House of Lords plus the Royal Assent.

....

....

Bowles v Bank of England [1913] 1 Ch 57

The principle in the case above was accepted and applied in this case by Parker J. The issue here was whether a resolution of the Committee of the House of Commons for Ways and Means could, once adopted by the House of Commons, authorize the Crown to levy and collect taxes before the annual Finance Bill had become an Act of Parliament.

The judge held that legislation was required before the Crown could levy and collect taxes and that a resolution was not equivalent to an Act of Parliament because it had not received the necessary assents.

....

The Parliament Acts 1911 and 1949 and the meaning of Act of Parliament

Under the **Parliament Acts 1911 and 1949**, bills may become Acts of Parliament without the assent of the House of Lords if the Lords fail within one month to pass a bill certified as a

Money Bill by the Speaker of the House of Commons or refuse in two successive sessions, whether of the same Parliament or not, to pass a public bill which has been passed by the Commons in those two sessions, provided that one year has elapsed between the date of the bill's second reading in the Commons in the first of those sessions and the date of the third reading in that House in the second of those sessions.

The only exception is a bill which seeks to extend the life of a Parliament for more than five years. Examples include the **Welsh Church Act 1914, Government of Ireland Act 1914, Parliament Act 1949, War Crimes Act 1991, European Parliamentary Election Act 1999, Sexual Offences (Amendment Act) 1999**, and the **Hunting Act 2004**.

....

Jackson v Attorney General [2006] 1 AC 262

The House of Lords, among other things, held that the purpose of the **Parliament Act 1911** was to restrict the power of the House of Lords to defeat bills which had been passed by the House of Commons. **Section 2(1) Parliament Act 1911** creates a parallel way in which any public bill introduced into the House of Commons can become an Act of Parliament. The **1911 Act** applies to any public bill and for this reason there is no basis for implying any exceptions beyond those expressly mentioned in the **1911 Act**. Accordingly, the **Parliament Act 1949** and the **Hunting Act 2004** are valid Acts of Parliament.

....

The legislative process

Revision tip

Especially when answering essay questions, students think that they can impress their examiners by writing all they know about parliamentary procedure, whether or not it is required to answer the question. Remember, all you really have to do in an examination is answer the questions. Do not give examiners more than they want. You will not get extra marks for doing so.

Most bills originate from within the government. The scope for legislative initiatives by individual MPs is very limited. The legislative process is in three stages. The first stage concerns the period before publication of the bill. The second stage is the passage of the bill through Parliament. The third stage concerns the coming into force of the Act after the bill has received the Royal Assent.

The allocation of time in the House of Commons

The allocation of time to parliamentary business in the House of Commons is achieved by Programme Motions, Programme Orders, and Closure Motions;

The legislative process
✷✷✷✷✷✷✷✷✷✷

Programme Motions in the House of Commons

A timetable for the passage of a government bill through the House of Commons is agreed by MPs when it receives its second House of Commons reading. This is done by tabling a Programme Motion.

Programme Orders in the House of Commons

A Programme Order gives effect to the agreed timetable proposed by the Programme Motion.

Closure Motions in the House of Commons

The Speaker of the House of Commons may close a debate and ask the House to vote on an issue. This is called a division. An MP may ask the Speaker to do this by tabling a Closure Motion which may require the support of at least 100 MPs. The discretion of the Speaker in this matter is absolute.

The role of back benchers: private members' bills

Public bills may be sponsored by individual members of the House of Commons or House of Lords. These are called **private members' bills** because they do not form part of the government's legislative programme. They are allocated a very limited amount of parliamentary time which seriously reduces their chances of becoming law. All that a member or Lord needs to provide is the short title by which the bill will be known and a long title which briefly describes what the bill does.

Private members' bills can by introduced by the Ballot, the Ten Minute Rule; and Presentation.

The Ballot

At the beginning of the parliamentary year a ballot is held to decide which of all the members who wish to introduce a bill will be allocated debating time. One day is usually allocated to the first seven bills drawn from the ballot. These are called Ballot Bills.

Ten Minute Rule

A bill introduced under this rule gives its sponsor ten minutes to speak in favour of the issue addressed by the bill. Another member may speak against it for ten minutes. This procedure is commonly used to raise awareness of an issue.

Presentation

Any member may introduce a bill in this way as long as he or she has previously given notice of their intention to do so. Members formally introduce the title of the bill but do not speak in support of it. These bills rarely become law.

Private members' bills introduced into the House of Lords

A similar procedure applies where private members' bills are introduced into the House of Lords. If it passes its House of Lords' stages it proceeds to the House of Commons if an MP is prepared to support it.

Raising objections to a private members' bill

Anyone who objects to a private members' bill can write to their MP or to a Member of the House of Lords or to a minister, if the bill has government support. Members of the public may lobby Parliament directly.

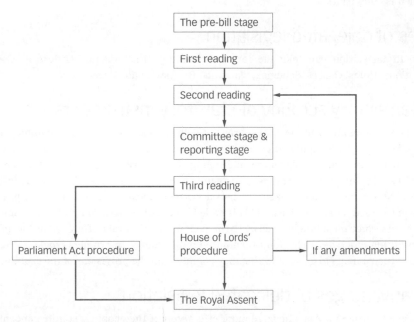

Figure 8.1 Public Bill procedure diagram

Private bills

Private bills are subject to the same procedural requirements as public bills. One important difference, however, is that the House of Lords may veto a private bill. There is also no Report Stage in the House of Lords for private bills. In addition, a Private Bill will not be debated at the second reading stage unless objections to its provisions have been raised. If there are objections a private bill is sent to the Opposed Bill Committee. If there are no objections it goes to the Unopposed Bill Committee.

After the committee stage the bill is reported to the House and its subsequent stages.

Delegated legislation

What is delegated legislation?

Parliament may give legislative powers to the executive by statute. Statutes which do this are called enabling Acts. Delegated legislation is law made by the executive when exercising these powers. The enabling Act contains general provisions and then empowers the executive to make more detailed law covering the subject matter of the relevant legislation. These take effect as if they are part of the enabling Act. An example of this is the **Criminal Justice Act 2003**. This empowers the Secretary of State to make codes of practice which the police use when issuing cautions.

Types of delegated legislation

Delegated legislation can take the form of Statutory Instruments, Orders in Council, Regulations, Rules, Orders, Schemes, Warrants, By-Laws, and Directions.

Parliamentary scrutiny of Statutory Instruments

Statutory Instruments form the largest group of delegated legislation. Many statutory instruments take effect on a stipulated date without parliamentary scrutiny. One of three parliamentary procedures may apply where an enabling Act requires a Statutory Instrument to be laid before Parliament. Some Statutory Instruments are laid before Parliament for information only. No further action is taken. Others take effect unless there is a motion or prayer of annulment passed by either House. This is called a *negative resolution procedure*. Statutory Instruments which must be approved by Parliament before they take effect follow the *affirmative resolution procedure*. The Joint Committee on Statutory Instruments looks at General Statutory Instruments to make sure that they comply with the provisions of the enabling Act.

The advantages of delegated legislation

Parliamentary time may be allocated more effectively if the enabling statute concentrates on the general principles and provisions. The executive takes responsibility for carrying these principles into effect by making detailed regulations as and when required. This is especially useful in emergencies or rapidly changing circumstances. Statutory Instruments often contain detailed provisions affecting local or technical issues requiring the kind of specialist expertise which can be found within departments of state. Because the process of making delegated legislation is quicker and less complex than passing or amending Acts of Parliament it promotes flexible government.

The disadvantages of delegated legislation

It undermines the separation of powers by giving too much legislative power to the executive especially where the rights and obligations of the general public are concerned. It makes the process of law-making less democratic by giving Parliament less time to scrutinize measures before they become law. It can lead to undesirable levels of sub-delegation especially where local authorities are empowered to make bylaws. Not enough parliamentary time is given to scrutinizing delegated legislation and there is simply too much delegated legislation for the general public to keep up with the law.

The jurisdictional question

Revision tip

Problem questions commonly focus on this issue. Remember that, in problem questions, you are not concerned with the political consequences of legislation or contextual issues. You are concerned with the legal principles governing the courts' powers to apply and interpret legislation.

Essay questions might ask you to consider contextual issues concerning the relationship between the courts and Parliament. This links up with the separation of powers (see chapter 4).

According to AV Dicey in Introduction to the Study of the Law of the Constitution (1885), the principle of parliamentary sovereignty means that Parliament has the right to make or unmake any law whatsoever and no person or body has the right to override or set aside legislation. The first part of the principle is positive. The second part is negative.

✓ *Looking for extra marks?*

There is considerable debate about whether, in the light of developments in EU law, devolution and the passing of the **Human Rights Act 1998**, Dicey's idea of parliamentary sovereignty is becoming increasingly outdated and irrelevant. See the key debates section for further reading.

If Parliament can make or unmake any law it likes, can Parliament alter its own constitution? It appears that Parliament does have this power.

Can Parliament alter its own constitution?

Parliament has the power to alter its own constitution for certain purposes.

....

Jackson v Attorney General [2006] 1 AC 262

The House of Lords had to decide whether the **Parliament Act 1949**, which amended the **Parliament Act 1911**, was invalid because it was passed without the consent of the House of Lords in accordance with the procedure contained in **s 2 Parliament Act 1911**. If the **1949 Act** were invalid the **Hunting Act 2004** would also be invalid. The House of Lords held that there is no constitutional principle, or principle of statutory interpretation, which prevents a legislature from altering its constitution in accordance with the provisions of a statute which empowers it to do so, for the purpose of altering the empowering statute.

....

The development of the rule that no person or body has the right to override or set aside legislation

In the constitutional turmoil of the seventeenth century there were suggestions that the courts might have the power to question the validity of an Act of Parliament if it was:

- against common right or reason, repugnant, or impossible to perform (*Dr Bonham's Case* (1610));
- against natural equity (*Day v Savage* (1615));
- contrary to the law of God in scripture (*R v Love* (1651)); and
- contrary to the rules of natural justice (*City of London v Wood* (1702)).

Challenges based on substance

In the United Kingdom there is no equivalent to the principle stated by Chief Justice Marshall in the United States Supreme Court's decision in *Marbury v Madison* (1803) that a statute which is repugnant to the constitution is void. In the Privy Council decision in *Madzimbamuto v Lardner Burke* (1969), Lord Reid said that while many might think that it would be morally or politically unconstitutional for Parliament to do certain things this does not diminish or undermine the legal power of Parliament to legislate. If Parliament chooses to do them, the courts cannot hold the resulting Act of Parliament invalid.

Cheney v Conn [1968] 1 All ER 779

Ungoed-Thomas J said that anything enacted in a statute cannot be unlawful. Statute is the highest form of law within the United Kingdom and it is not for a court to say that an Act of Parliament is illegal.

See also *Mortensen v Peters* (1906) and *R v Jordan* (1967).

Procedural challenges: the enrolled bill rule

The enrolled bill rule is that the courts have no jurisdiction, once a bill has become an Act, to consider:

1. the way in which a bill is introduced into Parliament and what happened either before or during its progress through Parliament; and
2. whether Parliament or its officers were misled by fraud.

These principles were laid down in:

- *Edinburgh & Dalkeith Railway v Wauchope* (1842);
- *Lee v Bude and Torrington Junction Railway* (1871); and
- *Pickin v British Rail Board* (1974).

Express and implied repeal

Revision tip

In problem questions you may be asked to consider whether the provisions of an Act of Parliament can be protected from subsequent changes. The first thing you must do is make sure that you understand the distinction between implied and express repeal.

An Act of Parliament overrides common law. Parliament changes statute law by the process of repeal. There are two types of repeal, namely, express repeal and implied repeal. Express repeal is a statement in an Act declaring that the provisions of an earlier statute are no longer in force or are replaced with the provisions of the new Act. Implied repeal is a common law rule. Laws LJ in *Thoburn v Sunderland City Council* (2003) said that implied repeal may occur where Parliament enacts successive statutes which on the true construction of each of them make irreducibly inconsistent provisions. In such a case the outcome is that the earlier statute is impliedly repealed by the later.

The way in which the courts perceive their jurisdiction changes with time. According to Avory J in *Vauxhall Estates Ltd v Liverpool Corporation* (1932) no Act of Parliament can effectively provide that no future Act shall interfere with its provisions. In *Ellen Street Estates, Limited v Minister of Health* (1934) Maugham LJ said that the legislature cannot bind itself as to the form of subsequent legislation. By this, he meant that it is impossible for Parliament to enact that, in a subsequent statute dealing with the same subject matter, there can be no implied repeal. If, in a subsequent Act, Parliament plainly says that an earlier statute is being to some extent repealed, effect must be given to that intention just because it is the will of the legislature.

There now seems to be an exception to the rule. In *Thoburn v Sunderland City Council* (2003) Laws LJ draws a distinction between ordinary and constitutional statutes. He went on to make the following points:

- A constitutional statute concerns the relationship between the citizen and the state and/ or fundamental human rights.
- Ordinary statutes may be impliedly repealed. Constitutional statutes may not.
- For the repeal of a constitutional statute, the court must find express words in the later statute which irresistibly show that Parliament intended to repeal the former constitutional statute.

Can the jurisdiction of the court over an Act of Parliament be enlarged?

There are some instances where courts seem willing to expand their jurisdiction over Acts of Parliament. These include:

- reference to parliamentary material in statutory interpretation;

- the use of entrenchment clauses and prospective formulae; and
- the **Human Rights Act 1998.**

Reference to parliamentary material in statutory interpretation

The courts do not normally permit parliamentary material to be used as evidence when interpreting statutes. This is partly based on **Article 9 Bill of Rights 1689** which provides that the freedom of speech and debates or proceedings in Parliament ought not to be impeached or questioned in any court or place outside of Parliament. There are now exceptions to this rule based on the following principles:

- subject to parliamentary privilege, parliamentary material may be allowed where:
  - legislation is ambiguous or obscure or leads to absurdity;
  - the material is a statement by a minister or sponsor of a bill and any additional parliamentary material necessary to understand such statements and their effect; and
  - the statements are clear;
- if Parliament enacts legislation after making clear statements in both Houses, it is appropriate to refer to parliamentary material if there is any ambiguity concerning the Act's nature and scope; and
- there is nothing to prevent material in parliamentary speeches being admitted as evidence where the court is considering not only the meaning of the provisions of the statute but also the intention behind it.

....

Pepper v Hart [1992] 3 WLR 1032

The first principle was determined by the House of Lords in this case.

The claimants challenged a decision of the Inland Revenue concerning assessment of tax. The assessment was based on **ss 61** and **63 Finance Act 1976**. The claimants alleged that these provisions were ambiguous. An enlarged Appellate Committee of the House of Lords chaired by the Lord Chancellor, Lord Mackay, had to decide whether parliamentary material could be used in aiding the interpretation of legislation.

It was held that parliamentary material may be used to assist in the interpretation of legislation in cases where such legislation is ambiguous or obscure.

....

R v Secretary of State for Foreign and Commonwealth Affairs, ex p Rees-Mogg [1994] QB 552

The second principle was determined by Lloyd LJ in this case.

The claimant sought judicial review of the Foreign Secretary's decision to ratify the **Treaty of European Union (1992)**. The claimant's evidence included large extracts from parliamentary

Can the jurisdiction of the court over an Act of Parliament be enlarged?

★★★★★★★★★★★

statements made by ministers which were reported in Hansard. The claimant relied on **Pepper v Hart**. The Secretary of State argued that **Pepper v Hart** did not apply. Judicial review was refused and **Pepper v Hart** was not applied because there were no ambiguities in the relevant statutes. But had there been any ambiguities it would have been appropriate to apply **Pepper v Hart**.

Marshall, in *Public Law* (1993) at p 402, said that *ex p Rees-Mogg* **(1994)** means that **Article 9 Bill of Rights 1689** protects Members of Parliament from civil liability for what they say in debates and parliamentary proceedings. It does not prevent judicial scrutiny of parliamentary material where the courts have to decide on the legal effect of resolutions of either House. He concluded that the courts have jurisdiction to consider parliamentary material where:

- this was necessary to uphold the will of the Queen in Parliament; or

- a statute refers to parliamentary proceedings or resolutions and it is necessary to refer to them to determine what the statutory provisions mean.

Lord Browne-Wilkinson, in the Privy Council decision in *Prebble v Television New Zealand Ltd* **(1995)**, said that the courts and Parliament recognize their respective constitutional roles. The courts will not allow any challenge to what is said or done within Parliament in performance of its legislative functions and protection of its privileges.

Entrenchment clauses and prospective formulae?

Revision tip

Make sure that you understand the difference between these formulae. This will help you spot them in an examination problem question and apply the correct law.

Entrenchment clauses and prospective formulae are statutory provisions, which aim to protect an Act of Parliament from amendment or repeal. Entrenchment clauses in a statute require a special procedure to be followed before an Act of Parliament can be amended or repealed. This can be in the form of a referendum or poll or two-thirds majority. An example of such a clause appears in **s 1 Northern Ireland Act 1998**. This provides that Northern Ireland will remain part of the United Kingdom until a majority of the people give their consent to a change in a poll.

✅ *Looking for extra marks?*

RFV Heuston, in *Essays in Constitutional Law* (1964), considers the legal effect of entrenchment clauses in many jurisdictions and suggests that, in some contexts, they may bind a legislature as to the manner and form of legislation. You should read about this and think about whether it is possible to bind the Westminster Parliament in the same way.

Can the jurisdiction of the court over an Act of Parliament be enlarged?
✳✳✳✳✳✳✳✳✳✳

A prospective formula seeks to protect a statute from amendment or repeal by saying that its provisions prevail over those of subsequent statutes or that future statutes shall be construed and have effect subject to it provisions. An example of such a formula appears in **s 2(4)** of the **European Communities Act 1972** which provides, among other things, that any enactment passed or to be passed shall be construed and have effect subject to the foregoing provisions of **s 2**.

Revision tip

When revising this topic it is worth referring to chapter 9 which expands on the constitutional implications of UK membership of the EU.

The Human Rights Act 1998

Section 3 Human Rights Act 1998 obliges the courts to interpret statutes in accordance with Convention Rights as far as it is possible to do so. **Section 4** gives the High Court in England and Wales the jurisdiction to issue a declaration of incompatibility. Moreover, **s 2** obliges the courts to take into account the decisions of the European Court of Human Rights when making decisions involving European Convention Rights. None of this affects the validity of an Act of Parliament and the Government is not bound by a declaration of incompatibility to amend incompatible legislation.

The judicial use of **ss 3** and **4** is illustrated by the House of Lords' decision in *Ghaidan v Godin-Mendoza* **(2004)**. In this case the House of Lords determined that, subject to the limitation of doing what is possible, **s 3** gives the courts jurisdiction to modify the meaning of words used in statutes. If the court finds that **s 3** requires this, it is bound only to interpret the statute in accordance with the underlying thrust of the legislation. The court is not bound to follow the exact form of words used in the Act. In this way a court can interpret any statute in a way which is compatible with Convention Rights while, as far as it is possible to do so, without crossing the constitutional boundaries preserved by **s 3**.

The courts have no jurisdiction to declare a statute invalid. But in *International Transport Roth GmbH v Secretary of State for the Home Department* **(2003)** Laws LJ said:

- the British system is moving away from parliamentary supremacy towards constitutional supremacy;

- although Parliament, subject to the European Union, has unlimited legislative powers, the common law now recognizes and endorses the notion of constitutional or fundamental rights;

- these rights are contained in the European Convention on Human Rights and Fundamental Freedoms incorporated as Convention Rights under the **Human Rights Act 1998**;

- this creates tension between legislative sovereignty and the vindication of fundamental rights;

- in reconciling the competing claims of parliamentary sovereignty and fundamental constitutional rights the courts, firstly, acknowledge the legislative supremacy of parliament subject to a rule of construction that fundamental rights will not be overridden by a statute unless the words used expressly and specifically show that it was the intention of Parliament to do so; and

- the courts, secondly, have to strike a balance between the claims of the democratic legislature and the claims of the constitutional right by determining and measuring the degree or margin of deference it pays to the democratic decision-maker.

Laws LJ went on to say:

- greater deference is to be paid to an Act of Parliament than to a decision of the executive or to a subordinate measure;

- there is more scope for deference where the European Convention requires a balance to be struck, and less where the right is unqualified;

- greater deference will be due to the democratic powers where the subject matter lies within their constitutional responsibility, and less when it lies within the constitutional responsibility of the courts; and

- greater or lesser deference will be due according to whether the subject matter lies within the expertise of the courts.

✔ Looking for extra marks?

There has been a substantial amount of case law on **s 3 Human Rights Act 1998**. It is a hot topic. You should, therefore, supplement your revision by referring to chapter 14 of this guide and your recommended standard textbook.

✱ Key cases

Case	Facts	Principle
Ellen Street Estates, Limited v Minister of Health [1934] 1 KB 590	The Court of Appeal had to decide whether the provisions of a statute could be impliedly repealed because of the provisions of an earlier statute.	The legislature cannot bind itself as to the form of subsequent legislation.
International Transport Roth GmbH v Secretary of State for the Home Department [2003] QB 728	Laws LJ discussed the effect of the Human Rights Act on statutory interpretation and the legal doctrine of the legislative supremacy.	Since the coming into force of the Human Rights Act, the common law now recognizes a distinction between constitutional or fundamental rights on the one hand and other kinds of rights on the other.

Key debates

****

Case	Facts	Principle
R (Jackson) v Attorney General [2006] 1 AC 262	The House of Lords had to decide whether the Parliament Act 1949 and the Hunting Act 2004 were valid Acts of Parliament.	The purpose of the Parliament Act 1911 was to limit the power of the House of Lords to block the bill which had been approved by the House of Commons. There is no constitutional principle, or principle of statutory interpretation, which prevents a legislature from altering its constitution, in accordance with the provisions of a statute which empowers it to do so, for the purpose of altering the provisions of the empowering statute.
Stockdale v Hansard (1839) 112 ER 1112	The Court had to decide whether the House of Commons, by its own resolution, could extend its privileges and immunities.	The Lord Chief Justice held that the privileges and immunities of Parliament could be extended only by legislation which required the separate and simultaneous estates of the House of Commons and the House of Lords as well as the Royal Assent.
Thoburn v Sunderland City Council [2003] QB 151	The question was whether the European Communities Act 1972 was capable of being impliedly repealed.	Ordinary statutes may be impliedly repealed. Constitutional statutes may not.

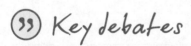 **Key debates**

Topic	'Professor Dicey's Contradictions'
Author/Academic	Iain McLean and Alistair McMillan
Viewpoint	In this article, the authors say: that Dicey is guilty of contradiction; that from a contradiction anything follows; that his passionate political views led him into dubious places; that Dicey's first position is untenable and unrealistic; that his second and third positions can be rescued but only by better arguments for popular sovereignty or entrenchment than Dicey ever offered.
Source	[2007] Public Law 435.

Topic	'The Paradox of Sovereignty: *Jackson* and the Hunt for a New Rule of Recognition?'
Author/Academic	James Allan
Viewpoint	Examines how the House of Lords judgment in *R (on the application of Jackson) v Attorney General* **(2006)**, on whether the **Hunting Act 2004** had been invalidly enacted under the **Parliament Act 1949** on the ground that the **1949 Act** had arisen from a misapplication of the s **2(1) Parliament Act 1911** procedure, illustrates the paradox of sovereignty identified by JL Mackie concerning the ability of a sovereign power to pass laws that limit its own sovereignty.
Source	[2007] Kings' Law Journal 1–22.

Topic	'Parliamentary Sovereignty under the New Constitutional Hypotheses'
Author/Academic	Jeffrey Jowell
Viewpoint	This article reviews the jurisdiction of the courts over Acts of Parliament in the light of the **Human Rights Act 1998** and other developments.
Source	[2006] Public Law 562.

Topic	'Bicameralism, Sovereignty and the Unwritten Constitution'
Author/Academic	Mark Elliott
Viewpoint	The author concludes by calling into doubt the nature of parliamentary sovereignty and by asking whether that concept exists – or should exist – in any absolute sense.
Source	[2007] IJCL 370.

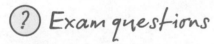

(?) Exam questions

Problem question

Assume that, in order to reduce the cost of the National Health Service to the taxpayer, the Health Services Act 2005 is passed which provides that all those receiving medical treatment must pay a fee according to a fixed scale contained in the Act. Section 2 provides that 'provisions of this Act are to take precedence over Acts passed or to be passed'. Section 3 provides that 'this Act is not to be amended or repealed unless the consent of the British Medical Council and the Royal College of Surgeons is obtained.

The scheme proves very unpopular and the Health Services (Amendment) Act 2006 is passed. This statute abolishes all fees. Neither the British Medical Council nor the Royal College of Surgeons is consulted.

Exam questions

****

Elizabeth has received a bill from her doctor following a blood transfusion. She refuses to pay, relying on the Health Services (Amendment) Act 2006. Her doctor relies on the Health Services Act 2005.

Advise Elizabeth as to whether she has to pay her doctor's bill.

Outline answers are included at the end of the book.

Essay question

Critically assess Dicey's assertions that Parliament can make or unmake any law it wishes and that an Act of Parliament cannot be overridden or set aside by the courts.

 Scan here

Scan this QR code image with your mobile device to see an outline answer to this question or log onto www.oxfordtextbooks.co.uk/orc/concentrate

#9
Tribunals

Key Facts

- Tribunals are an important part of the British justice system.
- They adjudicate and resolve interpersonal disputes as well as those involving the individual and the state.
- Until 2007 tribunals were not organized within a single framework but were set up by statute, were administered by public bodies forming part of the executive, and often acted as an appeal system from decisions made by a public body.
- In *Tribunals for Users – One System, One System One Service* (2001) Sir Andrew Leggatt said that there should be a single tribunal system, independent of the executive, administered by the Tribunal Service and these recommendations were accepted in the White Paper *Transforming Public Services: Complaints, Redress and Tribunals* (2004).
- **Part 1** of the **Tribunals Courts and Enforcement Act 2007** created a unified system consisting of two tribunals called the First-tier Tribunal and the Upper Tribunal staffed by the tribunal judiciary under a Senior President and enhanced the supervisory role of the Administrative Justice and Tribunal Council.
- Since 1 April 2011 administrative support for tribunals is provided by the Courts and Tribunal Service.
- Economy, speed, informality, and specialist expertise are some of the perceived advantages of tribunals.
- Lack of publicity, poor quality of investigation, the possibility of political interference, the danger that complex points of law may be considered by unqualified persons, and the unavailability of funding are some of the perceived disadvantages of tribunals.

> *Revision Tip*
>
> This topic links up with rule of law (chapter 3), separation of powers (chapter 4), judicial review, (chapters 11 and 12), and human rights (chapter 14) and may be combined with any of them in examination questions. You should therefore revise the material in this chapter in conjunction with these topics.

What is a tribunal?

> *Revision Tip*
>
> Essay type questions in particular may ask you to define and explain basic terminology. You should, at this point, be able to say what a tribunal is and point out both the similarities and the differences between courts and tribunals.

A tribunal is a body established to settle certain types of dispute. In some contexts, 'tribunal' and 'court' are capable of meaning the same thing. A tribunal may be a court in the sense that it exercises compulsory jurisdiction given to it by statute to resolve disputes between private individuals, as well as between the citizen and the state and regulate the rights and obligations of citizens. Some tribunals, like the Employment Appeal Tribunal and the Upper Tier Tribunal, are courts of record. But arbitrators, committees of clubs, and professional and university disciplinary bodies are sometimes called domestic tribunals. Their functions are quasi-judicial. They affect the rights of citizens. However, they are not courts. As far as statutory tribunals are concerned there are important differences between tribunals and the courts. Their jurisdiction is specific. Their procedure is informal.

The origin and development of tribunals

> *Revision Tip*
>
> The links between this topic and the rule of law and separation of powers is particularly important here. Review the contents of chapters 3 and 4 and identify the separation of powers and rule of law issues which arise.

Specialist statutory tribunals were set up as they were needed throughout the twentieth century. Their original aim was to provide an informal setting for the resolution of disputes between the individual and the state concerning administrative decisions. Cases were often adjudicated by non-lawyers and each tribunal had its own procedure. The parties to a dispute were allowed to represent themselves. Over the years the use of tribunals was extended to include interpersonal disputes especially in employment rights.

The ever-increasing use of tribunals led to criticism. Lord Hewart CJ, in a book called *The New Despotism* (1929), said that tribunals were contrary to the rule of law and violated the separation of powers because they gave the executive too much adjudicative power. The Donoughmore-Scott Committee was set up in 1932 but did not really address this issue. In 1957 the Franks Committee conducted a review of the statutory tribunal system and made a number of recommendations. It said that tribunals should be open, fair, and impartial. It also recommended the formation of what eventually became the Council on Tribunals to make sure that tribunals exercised their powers properly. Sir Andrew Leggatt was subsequently commissioned to review tribunals. His report, entitled *Tribunals for Users – One System, One Service*, was published in August 2001. He observed that the development of tribunals had not been coherent, that individual tribunals were set up by and usually administered by government departments, and that there was a wide variety of approach and practice. He concluded that statutory tribunals were both inefficient and not best capable of delivering just results. He recommended a restructuring of the tribunals into a single, independent system to be administered by a Tribunals Service. This was followed by a more general government review on public services in 2004, which looked at dispute resolution as a whole between citizen and the state.

✅ Looking for extra marks?

Essay questions demand evidence of wide reading and independent research. You should acquaint yourself with current academic and judicial perspective by reading your recommended textbook.

Establishment of the First-tier Tribunal and the Upper Tribunal

Revision Tip

Develop an awareness and comprehensive knowledge of the present system of tribunals and the personnel responsible for them. Again, consider the separation of powers and rule of law implications especially with regard to judicial independence.

The **Tribunals, Courts and Enforcement Act 2007** established the First-tier Tribunal and the Upper Tribunal. The First-tier Tribunal and the Upper Tribunal have judges assigned to them. The Senior President of Tribunals presides over both of the First-tier Tribunal and the Upper Tribunal. The Upper Tribunal is a superior court of record and, in many respects, has the same rights, privileges, and powers as the High Court in England and Wales. The First-tier Tribunal is organized into the following chambers: the Social Entitlement Chamber; the War Pensions and Armed Forces Compensation Chamber; the Health, Education and Social Care Chamber; the Tax Chamber; the General Regulatory Chamber; and the Immigration and Asylum Chamber. The Upper Tribunal is organized into the Administrative Appeals Chamber; the Tax and Chancery Chamber; the Lands Chamber; and the Immigration and Asylum Chamber of the Upper Tribunal.

Senior President of Tribunals

The office of Senior President of Tribunals was created by the **Tribunals, Courts and Enforcement Act 2007**. The Senior President of Tribunals is concerned with the First-tier Tribunal, the Upper Tribunal, employment tribunals, and the Employment Appeal Tribunal. The functions of the Senior President of Tribunals include laying before Parliament written representations on matters that appear to him to be matters of importance relating to tribunal members, or otherwise to the administration of justice by tribunals. The Senior President of Tribunals is also responsible for representing the views of tribunal members to Parliament, to the Lord Chancellor/Secretary of State for Justice and to ministers of the Crown generally. He or she must take into account the need for tribunals to be accessible, the need for proceedings before tribunals to be fair and to be handled quickly and efficiently, the need for members of tribunals to be experts in the subject matter of, or the law to be applied in, cases in which they decide matters, and the need to develop innovative methods of resolving disputes that are of a type that may be brought before tribunals.

Composition of tribunals and appointments

The responsibility for constituting the chambers of the First-tier and the Upper Tribunal rests with the Lord Chancellor/Secretary of State for Justice and the Senior President of Tribunals. Each chamber has a Chamber President appointed by the Lord Chancellor/Secretary of State for Justice and the Senior President of Tribunals.

Tribunals Service/HM Courts and Tribunal Service

The Tribunals Service was created in April 2006 as an executive agency of the Ministry of Justice, with the aim of establishing a unified administration for the tribunals system. Only the tribunals included in the First-tier Tribunal and the Upper Tribunal fall under the remit of the Tribunals Service, with other tribunals, such as the Residential Property Tribunal, remaining outside the Tribunals Service.

In March 2010 it was announced that the Ministry of Justice would be moving to bring together Her Majesty's Courts Service and the Tribunals Service into a new single organization with the aim of creating a new single organization for the efficient delivery of access to justice. This was done in 2011. Administrative support to tribunals is now provided by HM Courts and Tribunal Service.

The Administrative Justice and Tribunals Council

The Administrative Justice and Tribunals Council (AJTC) was set up by the **Tribunals, Courts and Enforcement Act 2007** to replace the Council on Tribunals. The AJTC consists of not more than 15 nor less than 10 appointed members. Of these, either two or three are appointed by the Scottish Ministers with the concurrence of the Lord Chancellor and the

Welsh Ministers; and either one or two are appointed by the Welsh Ministers with the concurrence of the Lord Chancellor and the Scottish Ministers. The remainder are appointed by the Lord Chancellor with the concurrence of the Scottish Ministers and the Welsh Ministers. The Lord Chancellor, after consultation with the Scottish Ministers and the Welsh Ministers, nominates one of the appointed members to be Chair of the AJTC. The Parliamentary Commissioner for Administration (the Parliamentary Ombudsman) is a member of the AJTC by virtue of his or her office. The Scottish Committee of the AJTC consists of the two or three members of the AJTC appointed by the Scottish Ministers (one being nominated by the Scottish Ministers as Chair) and three or four other members, not being members of the AJTC, appointed by the Scottish Ministers. The Parliamentary Ombudsman and the Scottish Public Services Ombudsman are members of the Scottish Committee by virtue of their office. The Welsh Committee of the AJTC consists of the one or two members of the AJTC appointed by the Welsh Ministers (one being nominated by the Welsh Ministers as Chair) and two or three other members, not being members of the AJTC, appointed by the Welsh Ministers. The Parliamentary Ombudsman and the Public Services Ombudsman for Wales are members of the Welsh Committee by virtue of their office.

The AJTC's functions with respect to tribunals include considering and reporting on any matter relating to listed tribunals that the AJTC determines to be of special importance, considering and reporting on any particular matter relating to tribunals that is referred to the AJTC by the Lord Chancellor, the Scottish Ministers and the Welsh Ministers, and scrutinizing and commenting on legislation, existing or proposed, relating to tribunals. 'Listed tribunals' are the First-tier Tribunal and Upper Tribunal established by the **2007 Act** and tribunals listed by orders made by the Lord Chancellor, the Scottish Ministers, and the Welsh Ministers. The AJTC must be consulted before procedural rules are made for any listed tribunal except the First-tier Tribunal and Upper Tribunal. The AJTC is represented on the Tribunal Procedure Committee that makes procedural rules for the First-tier Tribunal and Upper Tribunal.

Judicial review and appeals

Revision tip

Apart from the rule of law and separation of powers implications you should now revise this subject in conjunction with the material on judicial review in Chapters 11 and 12.

First-tier Tribunal

The First-tier Tribunal may review a decision made by it on a matter in a case, other than a decision that is an excluded decision. The First-tier Tribunal's power in relation to a decision is exercisable of its own initiative, or on application by a person who has a right of appeal in respect of the decision. Where the First-tier Tribunal has reviewed a decision, the First-tier

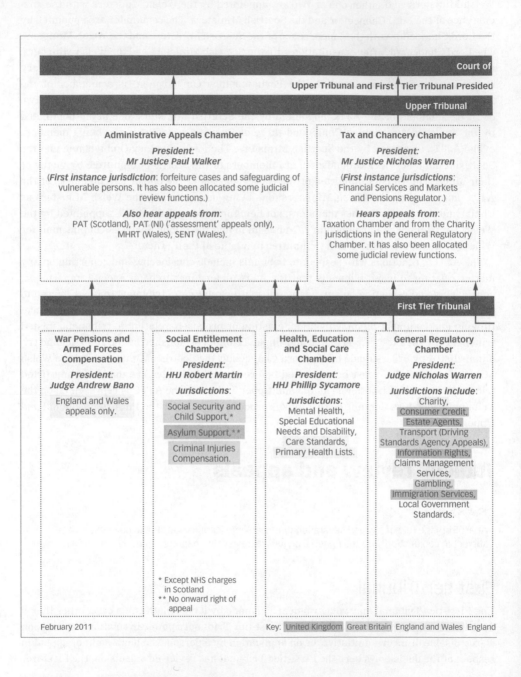

Court of

Upper Tribunal and First Tier Tribunal Presided

Upper Tribunal

Administrative Appeals Chamber

President:
Mr Justice Paul Walker

(*First instance jurisdiction*: forfeiture cases and safeguarding of vulnerable persons. It has also been allocated some judicial review functions.)

Also hear appeals from:
PAT (Scotland), PAT (NI) ('assessment' appeals only), MHRT (Wales), SENT (Wales).

Tax and Chancery Chamber

President:
Mr Justice Nicholas Warren

(*First instance jurisdictions*:
Financial Services and Markets and Pensions Regulator.)

Hears appeals from:
Taxation Chamber and from the Charity jurisdictions in the General Regulatory Chamber. It has also been allocated some judicial review functions.

First Tier Tribunal

War Pensions and Armed Forces Compensation

President:
Judge Andrew Bano

England and Wales appeals only.

Social Entitlement Chamber

President:
HHJ Robert Martin

Jurisdictions:

Social Security and Child Support,*

Asylum Support,**

Criminal Injuries Compensation.

Health, Education and Social Care Chamber

President:
HHJ Phillip Sycamore

Jurisdictions:
Mental Health, Special Educational Needs and Disability, Care Standards, Primary Health Lists.

General Regulatory Chamber

President:
Judge Nicholas Warren

Jurisdictions include:
Charity, Consumer Credit, Estate Agents, Transport (Driving Standards Agency Appeals), Information Rights, Claims Management Services, Gambling, Immigration Services, Local Government Standards.

* Except NHS charges in Scotland
** No onward right of appeal

February 2011

Key: United Kingdom Great Britain England and Wales England

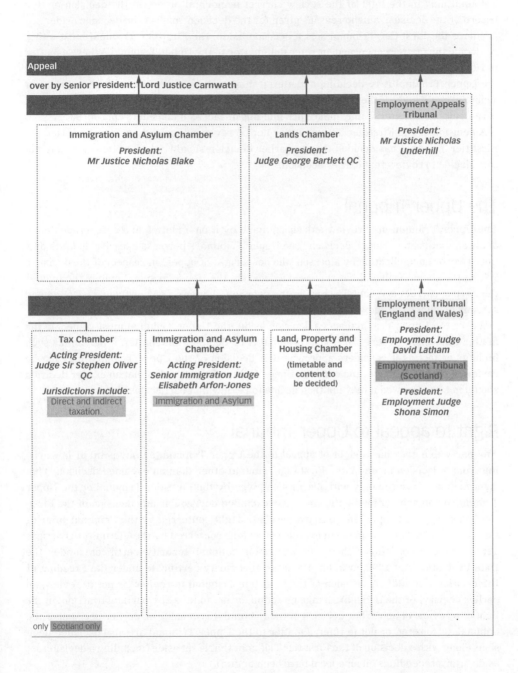

Appeal

over by Senior President: Lord Justice Carnwath

Immigration and Asylum Chamber

President:
Mr Justice Nicholas Blake

Lands Chamber

President:
Judge George Bartlett QC

Employment Appeals Tribunal

President:
Mr Justice Nicholas Underhill

Tax Chamber

Acting President:
Judge Sir Stephen Oliver QC

Jurisdictions include:
Direct and indirect taxation.

Immigration and Asylum Chamber

Acting President:
Senior Immigration Judge Elisabeth Arfon-Jones

Immigration and Asylum

Land, Property and Housing Chamber

(timetable and content to be decided)

Employment Tribunal (England and Wales)

President:
Employment Judge David Latham

Employment Tribunal (Scotland)

President:
Employment Judge Shona Simon

only Scotland only

Tribunal may in the light of the review correct accidental errors in the decision or in a record of the decision, amend reasons given for the decision, and set the decision aside.

Where the First-tier Tribunal sets a decision aside, the First-tier Tribunal must either re-decide the matter concerned, or refer that matter to the Upper Tribunal. Where a matter is referred to the Upper Tribunal, the Upper Tribunal must re-decide the matter. Where the Upper Tribunal is re-deciding a matter, it may make any decision which the First-tier Tribunal could make if the First-tier Tribunal were re-deciding the matter. Where a tribunal is re-deciding a matter, it may make such findings of fact as it considers appropriate.

A decision of the First-tier Tribunal may not be reviewed more than once, and once the First-tier Tribunal has decided that an earlier decision should not be reviewed it may not then decide to review that earlier decision.

The Upper Tribunal

The Upper Tribunal may review a decision made by it on a matter in a case, other than a decision that is an excluded decision. The Upper Tribunal's power is exercisable of its own initiative, or on application by a person who has a right of appeal in respect of the decision. Where the Upper Tribunal has reviewed a decision, the Upper Tribunal may in the light of the review correct accidental errors in the decision or in a record of the decision, amend reasons given for the decision, and set the decision aside.

Where the Upper Tribunal sets a decision aside, the Upper Tribunal must re-decide the matter concerned. Where the Upper Tribunal is re-deciding the matter, it may make such findings of fact as it considers appropriate. A decision of the Upper Tribunal may not be reviewed more than once, and once the Upper Tribunal has decided that an earlier decision should not be reviewed it may not then decide to review that earlier decision.

Right to appeal to Upper Tribunal

Any party to a case has a right of appeal to the Upper Tribunal on any point of law aris-ing from a decision made by the First-tier Tribunal other than an excluded decision. That right may be exercised only with permission given by the First-tier Tribunal or the Upper Tribunal on an application by the party. An 'excluded decision' is any decision of the First-tier Tribunal on an appeal made in exercise of a right conferred by the Criminal Injuries Compensation Scheme or made in exercise of a right conferred by the Victims of Overseas Terrorism Compensation Scheme or against a national security certificate under the **Data Protection Act 1998**, or against a national security certificate under the **Freedom of Information Act 2000**. A decision of the First-tier Tribunal to review, or not to review, an earlier decision of the tribunal, to take no action, or not to take any particular action, in the light of a review of an earlier decision of the tribunal, to set aside an earlier decision of the tribunal, or to refer, or not to refer, a matter to the Upper Tribunal are also excluded deci-sions along with a decision of the First-tier Tribunal that is set aside (including a decision set aside after proceedings on an appeal have been begun).

If the Upper Tribunal, in deciding an appeal, finds that the making of the decision concerned involved the making of an error on a point of law, the Upper Tribunal may (but need not) set aside the decision of the First-tier Tribunal, and if it does, must either remit the case to the First-tier Tribunal with directions for its reconsideration, or re-make the decision. If the Upper Tribunal remits the case to the First-tier Tribunal, it may also direct that the members of the First-tier Tribunal who are chosen to reconsider the case are not to be the same as those who made the decision that has been set aside and give procedural directions in connection with the reconsideration of the case by the First-tier Tribunal.

If the Upper Tribunal re-makes the decision, it may make any decision which the First-tier Tribunal could make if the First-tier Tribunal were re-making the decision, and may make such findings of fact as it considers appropriate.

Upper Tribunal's judicial review jurisdiction

The Upper Tribunal has power, in cases arising under the law of England and Wales or under the law of Northern Ireland, to grant the following kinds of relief: a mandatory order; a prohibiting order; a quashing order; a declaration; an injunction. This power may be exercised by the Upper Tribunal if certain conditions are met, or the tribunal is authorized to proceed even though not all of those conditions are met.

Relief granted by the Upper Tribunal has the same effect as the corresponding relief granted by the High Court on an application for judicial review, and is enforceable as if it were relief granted by the High Court on an application for judicial review.

In deciding whether to grant a mandatory order, a prohibiting order, or a quashing order, the Upper Tribunal must apply the principles that the High Court would apply in deciding whether to grant that relief on an application for judicial review. In deciding whether to grant a declaration or an injunction, the Upper Tribunal must apply the principles that the High Court would apply in deciding whether to grant that relief on an application for judicial review.

✅ Looking for extra marks?

You should read the case and articles recommended below especially *R (Cart) v The Upper Tribunal* which is currently before the Supreme Court.

The advantages and disadvantages of tribunals

Revision tip

Essay questions often ask students to look at the advantages and disadvantages of tribunals so you should spend some time revising this while taking a balanced approach.

Advantages

Effective use of time

The procedures adopted by tribunals mean that cases can be dealt with relatively quickly thus ensuring a speedy determination of a citizen's rights and entitlements.

Expense

Tribunals do not normally charge court fees and the indemnity rule does not apply, which means that the parties to a dispute only pay for their own costs.

Informal and flexible procedure

Informality and flexibility mean that the parties to a dispute may represent themselves more effectively and tribunals can respond more quickly and easily to the circumstances surrounding each individual case.

Expertise

Those who adjudicate in tribunals have the opportunity to gain specialist in-depth knowledge of their subject matter.

Lessening the caseload of the courts

Tribunals prevent the courts being clogged up with an unnecessarily high caseload.

Respect for the privacy of the parties

Tribunal cases can be heard in private.

Disadvantages

Lack of openness

In some cases there may be doubts about whether tribunals are sufficiently and openly independent.

Unavailability of state funding

Community Legal Service funding is not available except in a small number of cases.

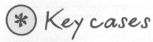 **Key cases**

Case	Facts	Principle
R (Cart) v Upper Tribunal and another [2011] QB 120	The claimant's former wife applied to the Child Support Agency for variation of a maintenance assessment payable by the claimant. Erroneously, the claimant was not informed of the application. The assessment was varied. When the claimant was notified of the variation he sought a revision which was refused. The First-tier Tribunal dismissed his appeal. The Upper Tribunal refused him permission to appeal in respect of his complaint that the Secretary of State had failed to give notice of the variation application. The claimant sought judicial review of that refusal, against which no appeal lay. A preliminary issue was ordered to be tried on the questions whether the designation of the Upper Tribunal as a 'superior court of record' by s 3(5) of the Tribunals, Courts and Enforcement Act 2007 meant that its decisions were not amenable to the supervisory jurisdiction of the High Court, and whether the decision which the claimant sought to challenge was amenable to judicial review. The Divisional Court held that although the phrase 'superior court of record' was not a reliable guide to which courts were immune from the supervision of the High Court, decisions of the Upper Tribunal, which was an alter ego of the High Court, were amenable to judicial review only on the grounds of an outright excess of jurisdiction or denial of procedural justice, neither of which applied to the claimant's case.	The designation of the Upper Tribunal as a "superior court of record" in s 3(5) of the Tribunals, Courts and Enforcement Act 2007 is not a reliable guide nor a definition of courts which are immune to judicial review. The supervisory jurisdiction of the High Court runs to statutory tribunals in both their old and new forms unless ousted by the plainest statutory language, which was lacking in the 2007 Act. The Act gives to the Upper Tribunal standing and powers akin to those of the High Court precisely because the tribunal is not a court of coordinate jurisdiction with the High Court and does not otherwise possess those powers. The possibility of control by the High Court of the legality of the Upper Tribunal's acts is therefore established.

❝ Key debates

Topic	'The Upper Tribunal in the Higher Courts'
Author/Academic	Chris Himsworth
Viewpoint	Examines two cases exploring the jurisdiction of the higher courts in England and Scotland to judicially review Upper Tribunal decisions not meeting the statutory criteria for an appeal.
Source	(2011) 15(1) Edinburgh Law Review 92–97.

Exam questions

****

Topic	'The Upper Tribunal's power to make determinations of fact on appeal from the First-tier Tribunal'
Author/Academic	Debra Morris
Viewpoint	Explores the jurisdictional issues raised by the **Tribunals Courts and Enforcement Act 2007**.
Source	(2009) British Tax Review 351.

Topic	'Decision making and appeals'
Author/Academic	Simon Rahilly
Viewpoint	Discusses the high percentage of correct decisions in adjudication in benefit claims as noted in the Secretary of State for Work and Pensions' report on the standard of decision making in the Department of Work and Pensions (DWP) which does not appear to accord with the growing number of appeals noted in a Tribunals Service report. Outlines the concerns from the Tribunals Service regarding the absence of representatives from the DWP at appeals and whether such non-attendance compromises the independence of the tribunals.
Source	(2010) 17(3) Journal of Social Security Law 141–142.

Topic	'Something old, something new: the new tribunal system'
Author/Academic	Edward Jacobs.
Viewpoint	Outlines the changes to the tribunal system brought in by the **Tribunals, Courts and Enforcement Act 2007** which introduce a system based on that of social security tribunals. Discusses the history of tribunals in the UK focusing on developments in 1908 under Lloyd George, the recommendations of the Franks Committee in the 1950s and Sir Andrew Leggatt's recommendations in his 2001 report. Sets out the structure and procedures of the revised tribunal system. Notes the procedure for appeal and review. Identifies a few potential problem areas
Source	(2009) 38(4) Industrial Law Journal 417–423.

 (?) Exam questions

Essay question 1

Critically assess whether or not the changes made by the Tribunals, Courts and Enforcement Act 2007 effectively deal Sir Andrew Leggatt's criticisms of tribunals in his report entitled *Tribunals for Users – One System, One Service* (2001).

Essay question 2

Explain the place, purpose, and functions of tribunals within the functions and organs of government within the United Kingdom.

 Scan here

Scan this QR code image with your mobile device to see outline answers to these questions or log onto www.oxfordtextbooks.co.uk/orc/concentrate

#10

European union law and institutions: constitutional implications

Key Facts

- The European Union is a supranational legal order based on treaties and general legal principles.

- The institutions of the European Union exercise legislative, executive, and judicial powers.

- The sources of European Union Law are Treaties, Regulations, Directives, Decisions, and Judgments of the European Court of Justice.

- Decisions of the European Court of Justice assert that human rights form part of the general principles of European Union law and **Article 6 Treaty on European Union (TEU)** has the effect of giving formal recognition that human rights, especially those protected by the **European Convention of Human Rights (ECHR)**, are part of EU law and are protected by the European Court of Justice.

- Regulations are 'directly applicable' in all Member States, while a Decision is binding upon those to whom it is addressed and a directive is binding, as to the result to be achieved, upon each Member State to whom it is addressed but leaves to the national authorities the choice of form and methods.

- The transfer by the states from their domestic legal systems to the Community legal system of the rights and obligations arising under the Treaty carries with it a limitation of their sovereign rights, against which a subsequent unilateral act incompatible with the concept of the Community cannot prevail while they remain members of the European Union.

- The effect of **s 2(1) and (4) European Communities Act 1972** is that the provisions of subsequent statutes are enacted without prejudice to the directly enforceable European Community rights of nationals of any Member State of the EEC.

- Substantive Community rights prevail over the express terms of any domestic law, including primary legislation, made or passed after the coming into force of the **1972 Act**, even in the face of plain inconsistency between the two.

Revision tip

Before reading this chapter, please refer to your study guides and other materials provided as part of your course to check coverage and emphasis. This chapter primarily focuses on the impact of European Union law on UK constitutional law issues.

Framework and institutions of the European Union

European Union Treaty framework since 1957

The **Treaty of Rome (1957)** established the European Economic Community. Other treaties of constitutional significance are the **Merger Treaty (1967)**, the **Single European Act (1987)**, the **Treaty on European Union (1992)**, the **Treaty of Amsterdam (1999)**, the **Treaty of Nice (2001)**, and the **Treaty of Lisbon (2007)**.

EU institutions

The main institutions are the Council of Ministers, European Commission, European Parliament, and the European Court of Justice. Other bodies like the Economic and Social Committee and the Committee of the Regions play important decision-making roles.

Sources of European Union law

Revision tip

In your plan you should revise this topic in conjunction with human rights, dealt with in chapter 14, and parliamentary sovereignty dealt with in chapter 8. Substantive European Union law, the institutional structure of the EU, and EU history is covered more fully in the EU Law Concentrate.

Other sources of European Union law are Regulations, Directives, Decisions, and Decisions of the European Court of Justice. These concern the interpretation of the treaties, regulations, and decisions, the recognition and development of general principles of law, and the development of doctrines of like direct effect.

General principles

General principles form a body of 'unwritten' law, stated and applied by the European Court of Justice and the Court of First Instance designed to assist it in its duties and to fill the gaps in the law. These General Principles are not to be confused with the fundamental principles of EU law as expressed in the **EC Treaty**. The general principles include proportionality, equality, legitimate expectation, legal certainty, the right to a hearing, duty to give reasons, right to due process, and legal professional privilege.

Human rights

The original **Treaty of Rome** lacked a catalogue of fundamental human rights. In some of its early case law, the ECJ denied that human rights were part of EC law. A turning point in its case law was *Stauder v City of Ulm* **(1969)** in which the European Court of Justice decided that human rights would be protected as part of the 'general principles of law'. **Article 6 TEU** has the effect of giving formal recognition that human rights, especially those protected by the **European Convention on Human Rights (ECHR)**, are part of EU law and are protected by the ECJ. Some of the earlier cases mentioned in this chapter can now be considered under the various articles of the **ECHR**.

The EU Charter of Fundamental Rights

The **European Union Charter of Fundamental Rights** sets out in a single text, for the first time in the European Union's history, the whole range of civil, political, economic, and social rights of European citizens and all persons resident in the EU. These rights are divided into six sections. These are Dignity, Freedoms, Equality, Solidarity, Citizens' rights, and Justice.

They are based, in particular, on the fundamental rights and freedoms recognized by the **ECHR**, the constitutional traditions of the EU Member States, the Council of Europe's Social Charter, the Community Charter of Fundamental Social Rights of Workers, and other international conventions to which the European Union or its Member States are parties.

Direct effect

The Treaty articles referred to below are those contained in the **Treaty of Rome (1957)** as amended by the **Treaty on European Union (1992)** which came into effect on 1 November 1993. The **1957 Treaty** articles appear in brackets.

Regulations

As defined in **Article 249(2) (ex 189(2)) EC, Regulations** are 'directly applicable' in all Member States.

Decisions

As defined in **Article 249(4) (ex 189(4))** a Decision is binding upon those to whom it is addressed.

Directives

Article 249(3) provides that a directive shall be binding, as to the result to be achieved upon each Member State to whom it is addressed but shall leave to the national authorities the choice of form and methods.

Member States must implement the provisions within the time-limit laid down in the directive. **Directives** have a different character from Regulations – they are important in the harmonization programme of the Community.

The authors of the Treaty did not intend that directives should have direct effect; however failure by Member States to fulfil their obligation under **Article 249(3)** led the European Court of Justice to apply the principle of direct effect (albeit to a limited extent). This was decided in the following case.

. . . .

Van Duyn v Home Office [1974] ECR 1337

Miss Van Duyn, a Dutch woman, was refused leave to enter the United Kingdom where she wished to take up a job with the Church of Scientology. Her action against the Home Office was based on community law guaranteeing the free movement of workers (**Article 48** and **Directive 64/221**). The High Court made a reference to the European Court of Justice.

The European Court of Justice held that **Article 3** of the Directive relied upon was capable of conferring rights on individuals which the courts of Member States were under an obligation to protect.

. . . .

Two further principles are important.

The first of these is that the binding nature of a directive, which constitutes the basis for the possibility of relying on the directive before a national court, exists only in relation to 'each Member State to which it is addressed'. It follows that a directive may not of itself impose obligations on an individual and that a provision of a directive may not be relied upon as such against such a person. This principle was determined by the European Court of Justice *Marshall v Southampton AHA* (1986) in which the Court determined that the claimant could rely on an anti-discrimination directive against the state regardless of the capacity in which the latter was acting.

The second is that the provisions of a directive can be relied on against organizations or bodies which are subject to the authority or control of the state or have special powers beyond those which result from the normal rules applicable between individuals. This was formulated by the European Court of Justice in *Foster v British Gas* (1991). The key issue here was whether the defendant was part of the State. The Court held that the directive could be relied upon.

Failure to transpose a Directive into national law

Article 10 (ex 5) provides that Member States shall make all appropriate measures, whether general or particular, to ensure fulfilment of the obligations arising out of this Treaty or resulting from action taken by the institutions of the Community. They shall facilitate the achievement of the Community's tasks. They shall abstain from any measure, which could jeopardize the attainment of the objectives of the Treaty.

....

Francovich v Italian State [1991] ECR I-5357

Directive 80/70 required Member States to set up guarantee funds in the event of an employer becoming insolvent. Italy failed to implement the Directive. F found himself denied the protection envisaged by the Directive.

It was held that it is a principle of Community law that the Member States are obliged to make good any loss and damage caused to individuals by breaches of Community law for which they can be held responsible.

This principle is subject to three conditions: (1) the result prescribed by the directive should entail the grant of rights to individuals; (2) it should be possible to identify the content of those rights on the basis of the provisions of the directive; and (3) there must be a causal link between the breach of the state's obligation and the loss and damage suffered by the injured parties.

The European Court of Justice decided that he could claim no effective rights as the provisions of the Directive lacked sufficient unconditionality.

....

These principles were applied by the European Court of Justice in *Dillenkofer v Federal Republic of Germany* (1997).

Breach of a Treaty provision by the national legislature

This was considered by the European Court of Justice in the following cases. The principle is discussed after the facts of both cases have been laid out.

....

Brasserie du Pecheur SA v Germany [1996] 1 QB 404

After the claimant (a French brewing company) claimed that it had been compelled to discontinue exports of beer to Germany because its beer did not comply with the purity requirement laid down in a German law, the Commission of the European Communities brought infringement proceedings against the Federal Republic of Germany. The Court of Justice of the European Communities held that the prohibition on the marketing of beers imported from other Member States which did not comply with the relevant national provisions was incompatible with **Article**

30 EEC Treaty. The plaintiff then brought an action against the Federal Republic of Germany seeking damages in respect of loss allegedly suffered as a result of the import restriction.

....

....

R v Secretary of State for Transport, ex p Factortame Ltd [1996] 1 QB 404

The applicants challenged, in an application for judicial review, the compatibility with Community law of **Pt II Merchant Shipping Act 1988**, which made registration of certain fishing vessels subject to conditions of nationality, residence and domicile of their owners, and deprived vessels ineligible for registration of the right to fish under the British flag. The Commission also brought infringement proceedings against the UK. The Court of Justice having held that the registration conditions were contrary to Community law, the applicants claimed from the UK damages in respect of expenses and losses allegedly incurred by them in consequence of the relevant provisions of the **Act of 1988**. One applicant was given leave to include a claim for exemplary damages. *The principles set out below apply to both cases*.

Member States must make good any damage suffered by individuals caused by a breach of Community law attributable to the state. This rule applies where the national legislature is responsible for the breach.

Where, in a field governed by Community law in which national legislatures had a wide discretion, there is a breach of Community law attributable to the national legislature, individuals suffering loss or injury have a right flowing directly from Community law to compensation where the rule of Community law breached is intended to confer rights on individuals, the breach of Community Law is sufficiently serious, in that the Member State has manifestly and gravely disregarded the limits of its discretion, and there is a direct causal link between the breach and the damage sustained.

....

Breach of a Treaty provision by the national administration

This was considered by the European Court of Justice in the following case.

....

R v Ministry of Agriculture, Fisheries and Food, ex p Hedley Lomas (Ireland) Ltd [1997] QB 139

Council Directive 74/577/EEC required Member States to ensure that certain animals were stunned by approved methods before slaughter. The Ministry refused to issue licences for the export to Spain of live animals for slaughter on the ground that, a number of slaughterhouses were not complying with the rules in the directive.

On the refusal of an application for an export licence, the applicant brought proceedings claiming a declaration that the refusal was contrary to **Article 34 EC Treaty** which prohibited quantitative restrictions on exports and measures having equivalent effect between Member States, and damages. The Ministry relied on **Article 36** whereby, **Article 34** was not to preclude prohibitions on exports on grounds of the protection of health and life of animals. The Queen's Bench Divisional Court referred to the Court of Justice of the European Communities for a **preliminary ruling** on the case.

The principle here was that a Member State cannot, on its own authority, unilaterally adopt corrective or protective measures designed to obviate any breach by another Member State of rules of Community law. A Member State has an obligation to compensate damage caused by breach of an Article where the rule of Community law infringed is intended to confer rights on individuals, the breach is sufficiently serious, and there is a direct causal link between the breach and the damage.

Incorrect transposition of a Directive into national law

This was determined by the European Court of Justice in *R v HM Treasury, ex p British Telecommunications Plc* (1996).

It was determined here that a Member State which incorrectly transposed a Community Directive into national law was liable to make reparation to individuals suffering loss and damage as a result thereof where the rule of law infringed was intended to confer rights on individuals, the breach was sufficiently serious and there was a direct causal link between the breach and the damage.

Liability for judicial acts

This was determined by the European Court of Justice in *Kobler v Austria* (2004).

Here the ECJ determined that the principle of state liability for damage caused to individuals as a result of breaches of Community law, for which the state is responsible, applies in principle to any breach of Community law. Liability extends to cases where the infringement stems from a decision of a court adjudicating at last instance. In such cases, the condition of liability that the breach has to be sufficiently serious is satisfied only if the breach is manifest. The factors to be taken into account for that purpose include the degree of clarity and precision of the rule infringed, whether the infringement is intentional, whether the error of law is excusable or inexcusable, the position taken, where applicable, by a Community institution and non-compliance by the court in question with its obligation to make a reference for a preliminary ruling under the third paragraph of **Article 234 EC**.

It is for each Member State to designate the court competent to determine disputes in such a matter.

The Lisbon Treaty

The **Treaty of Lisbon 2007** made significant amendments to the **EC Treaty** and the **Treaty on European Union (Maastricht) 1992**. The purpose of the treaty was to provide a unified legal framework for the EU. It gives the European Parliament and National Parliaments more influence over decision-making processes. EU citizens have greater access to information about the decision-making process at ministerial level and more influence over the content of new EU laws. This is called the 'Citizens' Initiative'. The Treaty also creates a more streamlined institutional structure designed to make it easier to combat crime, terrorism, and human trafficking. From a human rights perspective the **Lisbon Treaty** gives greater weight to the **EU Charter of Fundamental Rights**. It also gave a clear statement as to the values and goals of the European Union. Diplomacy, security, trade, and humanitarian aid are coordinated across the EU by officials holding newly created posts and there is now diplomatic and consular protection for all EU citizens travelling abroad. In the event of natural or man-made disasters the EU is now better equipped to make a coordinated effort to provide assistance.

European Union law in the UK: constitutional implications

Revision Tip

You should reconsider the doctrine of parliamentary sovereignty outlined in chapter 8 and assess its compatibility with the principle of the supremacy of European Union law presented here.

If there is conflict between European Union law and national law which prevails? According to the European Court of Justice the European Community is a new legal order of international law for the benefit of which the States have limited their sovereign rights and a legal system which forms an integral and binding part of the legal systems of Member States involving a permanent transfer of rights and obligations.

Any subsequent unilateral act which is incompatible with the concept of the Community cannot prevail. This was determined by the European Court of Justice in *NV Algemene Transport-Expedite Onderneming van Gend en Loos v Nederlandse Administratie der Belastigen* **(1963)** and *Costa v ENEL* **(1964)**. The English courts first considered the effect of this doctrine on the sovereignty of Parliament in the following case.

....

Blackburn v Attorney General [1971] 2 All ER 1380

The claimant brought two actions against the Attorney General claiming declarations to the effect that, by signing the Treaty of Rome, Her Majesty's Government would irreversibly surrender in part the sovereignty of the Queen in Parliament and in so doing would be acting in breach of the law. Eveleigh J upheld the order of the master striking out the statements of claim as disclosing no reasonable causes of action. The claimant appealed to the Court of Appeal. Lord Denning said that although, in theory, Parliament cannot bind its successors and declare an Act of Parliament to be irreversible, legal theory must, at times, give way to practical politics and that sovereignty is a political fact for which no purely legal authority can be constituted.

The declarations were refused.

....

The United Kingdom joined the European Community on 1 January 1973 under the terms of the **Treaty of Accession 1972**. This treaty was incorporated into UK law by the **European Communities Act 1972**. The effect of **ss 2 and 3** of the Act are to give legal effect in England to any rights and obligations created by the EC treaties and make available any remedies or procedures provided by the treaty without question.

This was determined by Lord Denning MR in *HP Bulmer Ltd and Another v J Bollinger SA and Others* (1974).

The Court of Appeal had to decide whether a matter concerning EC rights should be referred to the European Court of Justice. Both the trial judge and the Court of Appeal refused to refer the matter on the ground that it was not necessary to do so.

While the **European Communities Act 1972** remains in force, European Union law is supreme. But ultimately sovereignty still lies with the Queen in Parliament because the **European Communities Act 1972** can be expressly repealed by the present or any future Parliament. Lord Denning MR in *Macarthies v Smith* (1979) said that if Parliament deliberately passed an Act intending to repudiate the **EC Treaty** expressly, the courts would have no choice but to follow the provisions of the Act.

The purposive approach to statutory interpretation

One consequence has been the development of a purposive approach to the interpretation of statutes. One example of this is *Pickstone v Freemans* (1989). Here, the Court of Appeal took a purposive approach to **s 1(2)(c) Equal Pay Act 1970** to allow reliance on the Section in harmony with **Article 119 EEC Treaty**. Similarly, in *Litster v Forth Dry Dock & Engineering Co Ltd* (1990) the House of Lords determined that Regulations enacted in 1981 were expressly enacted for the purpose of complying with **Council Directive 77/187/ EEC** which provides for the safeguarding of employees' rights on the transfer of a business. The courts of the United Kingdom are under a duty to give a purposive construction to the Regulations in a manner which would accord with the decisions of the European Court of Justice on the Directive.

Factortame and sovereignty of Parliament

In *R v Secretary of State for Transport, ex p Factortame Ltd* (1990) (*Factortame (No 1)*) the High Court requested a preliminary ruling from the European Court of Justice (ECJ) to determine the compatibility of the **Merchant Shipping Act 1988** with the **EC Treaty**. As the ruling would take some two years to be given and in the meantime the applicants would suffer serious loss if they were unable to operate their vessels, interim relief in the form of temporary injunctions were sought. The High Court granted an interim order against the Crown that pending the final determination of the cases, the relevant parts of the **1988 Act** be disapplied in relation to the applicants and that the registration under the **Merchant Shipping Act 1994** continue.

The Secretary of State appealed and the Court of Appeal reversed the decision of the High Court. The Court of Appeal held as a matter of English law that the English courts had no jurisdiction to disapply an Act of Parliament. This conclusion was based on the presumption that an Act of Parliament was compatible with EC law until it is declared to be incompatible. The conclusion was also based on an old common law rule that an injunction cannot be granted against the Crown.

The House of Lords subsequently agreed with the Court of Appeal. The House of Lords referred to the ECJ the question of whether there was an overriding principle of EC law, that a national court was under an obligation to provide an effective interlocutory remedy to protect rights, having direct effect under EC law where a seriously arguable claim to such rights was advanced and the party claiming those rights would suffer irredeemable damage if he were not effectively protected in the meantime.

The ECJ replied first to the question referred to it by the House of Lords. The reply was that any rule of national law, which acts as the sole obstacle to interim relief being granted in a case concerning EC law, must be set aside. In response, the House of Lords restored the interim order granted by the High Court, which disapplied the relevant provisions of the **Merchant Shipping Act**.

Later, the ECJ delivered a ruling to the earlier reference from the High Court. The ECJ said that the system governing the regulation of British fishing vessels in the **1988 Act** was contrary to EC law.

. . . .

Equal Opportunities Commission v Secretary of State for Employment
[1994] 1 All ER 901

The Equal Opportunities Commission claimed that the provisions of the **Employment Protection (Consolidation) Act 1978** resulted in indirect discrimination against women which was contrary to EC law in particular **Article 119 EC** and **Directives of Equal Pay and Equal Treatment**.

The House of Lords made a declaration that the threshold provisions breached EC law.

. . . .

Following *Factortame (No 1)* substantive Community rights prevail over the express terms of any domestic law, including primary legislation, made or passed after the coming into force of the **1972 Act**, even in the face of plain inconsistency between the two. This was determined by Laws LJ in the Administrative Court's decision in *Thoburn v Sunderland City Council* **(2003)** (see key cases).

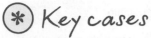 Key cases

Case	Facts	Principle
Francovich v Italy [1993] 2 CMLR 66	Italy had failed to implement Council Directive 80/987 relating to the protection of employees in the event of the insolvency of their employer. P was an employee in a company which became insolvent and which owed him a substantial amount of unpaid salary which it was unable to pay. Under the Directive, Italy should have established a guarantee fund to ensure employees a certain minimum protection in cases such as this. P therefore sued in the Italian court for compensation from the Italian Government on the basis that it was at fault in not having implemented the Directive.	The European Court of Justice decided that he could claim no effective rights as the provisions of the Directive lacked sufficient unconditionality.
NV Algemene Transport-Expeditie Onderneming van Gend en Loos v Nederlandse Administratie der Belastingen [1963] ECR 1	The Tariefcommissie, a Dutch administrative tribunal, made a reference to the European Court under Article 177 Treaty of Rome 1957.	The constitutional principle here is that the European Community is a new legal order with sovereign powers.
R v Secretary of State for Employment ex p Equal Opportunities Commission [1995] 1 AC 1	The House of Lords had to consider, among other things, whether it had jurisdiction to declare a UK statute incompatible with EU law.	The Divisional Court had jurisdiction to declare that primary legislation was incompatible with Community law.
R v Secretary of State for Transport, ex p Factortame Ltd (No 1) [1990] 2 AC 85	The House of Lords had to consider its jurisdiction to disapply the provisions of a UK statute which was incompatible with EU law.	Part II of the 1988 Act was unambiguous. If the court were to order the Secretary of State to treat F as entitled to registration and F were unable to prove they were entitled to registration in the European Court, interim relief would have given F rights which contravened parliamentary intention and deprived British fishing vessels of a proportion of the quotas available.

Key debates

✷✷✷✷✷✷✷✷✷✷✷✷✷

Case	Facts	Principle
Thoburn v Sunderland City Council [2003] QB 151	In four appeals the issue before the court concerned the introduction in accordance with the policy of the European Union of compulsory systems of metric weights and measures.	The common law recognized a category of constitutional statutes, and the fundamental legal basis of the United Kingdom's relationship with the EU rested with domestic rather than European legal powers.

 **Key debates**

Topic	**'Oh Brave new world! Lisbon Enters into Force'**
Author/Academic	Editorial
Viewpoint	Reports on the entry into force on 1 December 2009 of the **Treaty of Lisbon 2007**, which amends the **EC Treaty** and the **Treaty on European Union (Maastricht) 1992** in order to provide a unified legal framework for the EU. Describes the key changes to different aspects of the EU which the **Lisbon Treaty** effects, noting in particular changes affecting justice, freedom and security, external policy, the EU institutions, and EU law.
Source	(2005) 30(2) European Law Review 165–189.

Topic	**'Effectiveness in the European Legal Order(s): Beyond Supremacy to Constitutional Proportionality?'**
Author/Academic	Malcolm Ross
Viewpoint	Reviews European Court of Justice case law on the principle of effectiveness of EU law.
Source	(2006) 31(4) European Law Review 476–498.

Topic	**'Parliamentary Sovereignty under Pressure'**
Author/Academic	David Vaughan
Viewpoint	Presents a paper given at the Society of Legal Scholars and UK Association for European Law conference, *The Impact of Thirty Years of EU Membership on UK Law*, held in London in May 2004.
Source	(2005) 16(3) European Business Law Review 511–517.

Exam questions

Problem question

Assume that a European Union Regulation is passed in 2007 which provides that all European Union citizens shall be entitled to a minimum wage to the equivalent of £10 per hour.

In 2009 the UK Parliament passes the Minimum Wage Act. This Act provides that there shall be a minimum wage of £5 per hour.

Assuming that the year is 2013, and that Ernest, who works as a cleaner, is paid £5 per hour. When he objects, his employers rely on the Minimum Wage Act 2009. Ernest relies on the European Union regulation.

Write a report advising Ernest as to whether the European Union Regulation or the Minimum Wage Act 2009 determines his rights.

Outline answers are included at the end of the book.

Essay question

With reference to decided cases, critically assess the nature and extent of governmental liability for no implementation of an EU Directive.

Scan here

Scan this QR code image with your mobile device to see an outline answer to this question or log onto www.oxfordtextbooks.co.uk/orc/concentrate

#11

Introduction to administrative law: the foundations and extent of judicial review

Key Facts

- Judicial review allows people with a sufficient interest to ask a judge to review the lawfulness of a decision of a public body carrying out its public functions and enactments where there is no right of appeal or where all avenues of appeal have been exhausted.

- Judicial review is based on the constitutional principles of the rule of law and the separation of powers.

- The defendant must be a public body, the subject matter of a claim must be a public law matter, and the claimant must have the right to claim.

- The court may refuse to exercise its jurisdiction on policy grounds.

- It may be necessary to consider whether judicial review has been limited or excluded by Parliament.

- Quashing orders, mandatory orders, and prohibiting orders must be claimed by judicial review procedure contained in the current **Civil Procedure Rules** and **s 31** of the **Senior Courts Act 1981**, as amended by the **Civil Procedure Act 1997** and the **Civil Procedure (Modification of the Senior Courts Act) Order 2004**. Declarations, injunctions, and damages may be sought by judicial review procedure.

What is judicial review?

Judicial review allows a High Court judge to examine the lawfulness of decisions made by public bodies carrying out their public functions and 'enactments'. 'Public' means that the body making the decision is governmental and/or its decisions concern the general population as in a decision affecting the public.

Judicial review and appeals

Judicial review is available where no right of appeal exists or where such rights are exhausted.

Revision Tip

In an examination question you may need to decide whether the decision in question is appropriately challenged by judicial review or by appealing against it. If so you must be prepared to explain fully the differences between judicial review and an appeal.

There are important differences between judicial review and an appeal. On appeal the claimant says that the decision of a lower court or tribunal is wrong mainly, but not exclusively, on points of law. The decision of the lower court or tribunal may be reversed. Other earlier decisions may be overruled. The appeal court or tribunal replaces the judgment of the lower court or tribunal with its own. Statutes providing an appeal process stipulate the court or tribunal which may hear the appeal as well as the procedure, time limits, and grounds of appeal.

Judicial review focuses on the way public bodies make their decisions. The basis of a judicial review claim is not that a decision is wrong, unless the decision is so wrong that no reasonable public body could have reached it. The claimant must bring his claim within narrow technical grounds. These are considered in chapter 12.

Lord Diplock, in the House of Lords' decision in *Council of Civil Service Unions v Minister for the Civil Service* (1985) classified the grounds as illegality, irrationality, and procedural impropriety. Instead of substituting its own judgment, as it would in an appeal, the court may, in a judicial review, declare the decision void (empty of legal effect) by making a quashing order, or order the public body to do something by making a mandatory order, or order the public body not to do something by making a prohibiting order, or make a declaration that the defendant has acted unlawfully. Judicial review cannot be used to reverse or overrule or replace a decision.

The constitutional context of the supervisory jurisdiction

Revision Tip

Review the chapters on the separation of powers and the rule of law in this guide (chapters 3 and 4). Focus on the relationship between the judiciary and the executive and note the link between judicial review and the third part of Dicey's definition of the rule of law.

Judicial review forms the supervisory jurisdiction of the High Court in England and Wales. Claims are made to the Administrative Court. The constitutional basis for this is the rule of law and separation of powers. Judicial review gives effect to the principle that government must be conducted according to law. Judicial independence is vital. Although the basis of jurisdiction is statutory, the principles governing the role of the judiciary and the exact nature and scope of the supervisory jurisdiction have been developed by the judges in decided cases.

✓ Looking for extra marks?

You should look again at what senior members of the judiciary have said about the constitutional principle of the rule of law and the separation of powers as well as the opinions of leading academics. Many of these are well summarized in the leading textbooks. Be able to compare and contrast their opinions.

Is judicial review appropriate?

Revision tip

The first part of an answer to a problem question should focus on whether the defendant is a public body, whether its decisions are public law matters, and whether the claimant has the right to bring a claim for judicial review.

Judicial review must be appropriate. The important questions are is the defendant a public body? And is the defendant's decision a public law matter? Both questions must be addressed.

Is the defendant a public body?

Revision tip

When answering a problem question look at the source of the defendant's powers. If the source of the defendant's powers is neither statute nor Royal Prerogative (see chapter 5) apply *Datafin* (1987) and analyse the nature of the defendant's functions comprehensively.

The defendant must be a **public body**. In this context public means that a body is governmental. Executive organs of government are public bodies and are in principle subject to judicial review. These include ministers, departments of state, and local authorities. A body's duties, powers, and sanctions are public if they affect the general population and can be imposed, without consent. Many other organizations perform public duties as well as regulatory functions. They may make decisions which directly or indirectly affect the public at large. They may also act judicially. Some of them may have government support and exercise compulsory jurisdiction. The jurisdiction of the court over such organizations was considered by the Court of Appeal in *Datafin* (1987).

....

R v Panel of Take-overs & Mergers, ex p Datafin [1987] QB 815

The Court of Appeal considered, among other things, whether the High Court had jurisdiction to subject the decisions of the Panel to judicial review.

On this issue the key principle is that where there is a dispute concerning whether a defendant is a public body, the court must consider at least the source of power; the nature of the body's duties; and, the consequences of the body's decisions. A body can be subject to judicial review if its source of power is not solely the consent of those over whom it exercises its powers provided it performs public law duties and it is supported by public law sanctions.

The Court of Appeal decided that the High Court did have jurisdiction to review the Panel's decision.

The Court of Appeal developed these principles further in the following case.

R v Disciplinary Committee of the Jockey Club, ex p Aga Khan [1993] 1 WLR 909

The Court of Appeal had to decide whether the Disciplinary Committee of the Jockey Club was subject to judicial review.

The key principle is that the court looks at the origin, history, constitution, and membership of an organization to determine if it is a public body. A body whose origin and constitution owes nothing to the exercise of governmental control may be subject to judicial review if it has been woven into the fabric of public regulation or a system of governmental control; or is integrated into a system of statutory regulation; or is carrying out functions normally performed by an organ of government; or is doing something which would be done by an organ of government if the body in question did not exist. A body will not be subject to judicial review if its powers are based on agreement; and effective private law remedies are available.

The Court of Appeal decided that The Jockey Club was not a public body and not subject to judicial review.

These principles were applied in **R (on the application of Mullins) v Jockey Club Appeal Board (2006)** where it was decided that a newly appointed Board, set up to hear appeals from the Disciplinary Committee was not subject to judicial review.

✔️ Looking for extra marks?

These issues have attracted a great deal of academic argument. You should consult your textbook and learning materials to explore these developments and the key cases below.

Abuse of process: is the claim a public law matter?

Revision tip
Remember that public bodies are potentially subject to all forms of civil proceedings.

If the public body's decision is a public law matter it must be challenged by judicial review or the claimant might be accused of abuse of process. Lord Diplock, in *O'Reilly v Mackman* (1983) said that it is contrary to public policy and an abuse of the process of the court for a claimant to bring a public law matter to court by way of ordinary civil procedure thereby avoiding the protection given to public authorities by judicial review procedure.

Abuse of process means that the claimant seeks to gain unfair advantage. In this context unfair advantage-means depriving a public body of the judicial protection given to it by judicial review procedure. The requirement that a claimant must seek permission to proceed with a claim for judicial review within three months of becoming aware of a public body's decision is one of the ways in which judicial review procedure aims to protect public bodies.

What should a claimant do to avoid an accusation of abuse of process?

The Court of Appeal in *Rye v Sheffield City Council* (1998) said that if it is unclear that a case is a public law matter, the claimant should seek judicial review to avoid an accusation of abuse of process. If the claimant chooses private law civil procedure and it is unclear whether judicial review is more appropriate, the court should ask whether permission would have been granted had the claimant asked for judicial review. If so, this indicates that no harm has been done to the interests judicial review protects. The court should consider transferring the case to the appropriate list before striking it out.

In *Clark v University of Lincolnshire and Humberside* (2000) the Court of Appeal said that flouting the protection given to public authorities by judicial review procedure is contrary to the overriding objective in **Part 1 Civil Procedure Rules** and that the claimant must help the court fulfil the overriding objective by acting reasonably and by not using procedure to gain unfair advantage. If the court is asked to review something and grant a discretionary remedy, the use of ordinary civil procedure is inappropriate. If a claimant chooses private law proceedings, to make a claim normally made by judicial review, because of delay, the court must ask whether the delay was justified. Unjustified delay can be a ground for refusal to grant a discretionary remedy and can be taken into account in an application for summary judgment in normal civil proceedings. If the court is asked to review something and grant a discretionary remedy, the use of ordinary civil procedure is inappropriate.

Exceptions to the rule

Collateral challenge is an exception to the rule in *O'Reilly v Mackman* (1983) recognized by the House of Lords in *Wandsworth LBC v Winder* (1985). The key principle is that it is not an abuse of process for someone to raise a public law matter as a defence in civil proceedings. The defence is a collateral challenge in a private law matter.

Does the claimant have the right to bring a claim for judicial review?

Revision tip

This topic should be covered in detail in an answer to a problem question where the defendant is a representative organization.

According to the **Pre-Action Protocol for Judicial Review** a person can bring a claim if they have sufficient interest in the matter. It is also possible for someone other than the claimant or defendant to take part in the claim as an interested party. **Part 54 Civil Procedure Rules** defines 'interested party' as anyone other than the claimant or defendant who is directly affected by the decision. 'Sufficient interest' was considered by the House of Lords in the following case.

....

IRC v National Federation of the Self-employed and Small Businesses [1982] AC 617

The House of Lords had to decide whether the National Federation of the Self-employed and Small Businesses had the right to bring a claim for judicial review against the IRC after it had decided not to collect income tax from casual Fleet Street newspaper workers.

The key principle is that the question of whether a person has sufficient interest should not be treated as a preliminary issue, but must be considered in the legal and factual context of the whole case. The merits of the challenge are an important, if not dominant, factor when determining whether a claimant has sufficient interest. The real question is whether the claimant has a potentially good case, and not whether his personal rights or interests are involved.

The House of Lords decided that the Federation had no claim because the IRC had acted within its powers.

....

In *R v Inspectorate of Pollution, ex p Greenpeace* (1994) and *R v Secretary of State for Foreign Affairs, ex p World Development Movement* (1995) the following key principles were formulated.

Where the claimant is a representative organization the court can take into account the reputation of the body; whether a significant number of its members are affected by a decision; and whether it is reasonable for the organization to claim on behalf of its members. Other significant factors include the importance of vindicating the rule of law; importance of the issue raised; likely absence of any other responsible challenger; nature of the breach of duty against which relief is sought; and the prominence of the organization in giving advice, guidance, and assistance.

Has judicial review been excluded by Parliament?

Revision Tip

In problem questions you may be asked to consider the effect of a provision in a statute which purports to limit or exclude the jurisdiction of the court to consider a case. Your understanding of judicial policy will be improved by considering the relevant case law.

By statute, Parliament may seek to exclude or limit judicial review. **Section 12 of the Tribunals and Inquiries Act 1992** provides that any provision in an Act of Parliament passed before 1 August 1958 that an order or determination shall not be called into question by a court, or any provision in any such Act which by similar words excludes any of the powers of the High Court, shall have no effect. Such provisions passed after 1 August 1958 are subject to the following rules.

Finality clauses

If a statute says that some decisions or orders 'shall be final' this means merely that there is no appeal. Judicial review remains unimpaired. This was determined by the Court of Appeal in *R v Medical Appeal Tribunal, ex p Gilmore* (1957). The key principle is that it would be contrary to the rule of law to give tribunals the power to determine their own jurisdiction and that the words used in a statute must be sufficiently clear to show that Parliament intended to exclude judicial review. The word final is not enough.

'Shall not be questioned' clauses

Some statutes say that an order or determination 'shall not be questioned in any legal proceedings whatsoever'. The effect of such provisions was considered by the House of Lords in *Anisminic v Foreign Compensation Commission* (1969). This case concerned a provision in the **Foreign Compensation Act 1950** which said that any 'determination by the Commission of any application made to them under this Act shall not be called in question in any court of law'.

The key principle is that a provision that a determination shall not be called in question in any court of law does not protect a determination which is made as a result of a mistake of law which is a nullity and can be quashed by the court. This includes anything amounting to grounds for judicial review.

This key principle was applied by the Court of Appeal in *R v Secretary of State for the Home Department, ex p Al-Fayed* (1997).

Section 44(2) of the British Nationality Act 1981 provided, among other things, that the decision of the Secretary of State concerning naturalization 'shall not be subject to appeal to, or review in, any court'. Lord Woolf MR held that there was an inference that Parliament did not intend to exclude judicial review in cases alleging unfairness or discrimination.

Time limit clauses – partial ousters

The stipulated time limit for bringing judicial review is three months. Sometimes statutes impose a shorter time limit, for example six weeks. Statutes may also limit the grounds for judicial review. Such clauses are generally upheld by the courts. Parliament's intention to impose such restrictions is sufficiently clear. This was determined by the House of Lords in *Smith v East Elloe RDC* (1956). The House of Lords had to consider whether a compulsory purchase order could be challenged on the ground that it was made unfairly and in bad faith in spite of a six weeks limitation period. Although the Law Lords expressed a variety of opinions, it was decided that the time limitation clause was effective to prevent judicial review. *Smith v Elloe RDC* was critically discussed by the Law Lords in *Anisminic v Foreign Compensation Commission*. After *Anisminic* it was suggested that time limitation clauses were no longer effective. This argument was rejected by the Court of Appeal in *R v Secretary of State for the Environment, ex p Ostler* (1977). Lord Denning stressed the point that such clauses were necessary to ensure efficient administration and economy. In subsequent cases like *R v Secretary of State for the Environment, ex p Kent* (1990) and *R v Cornwall CC, ex p Huntingdon* (1994) such clauses were upheld on the basis that Parliament's intention was sufficiently and clearly expressed.

Summary

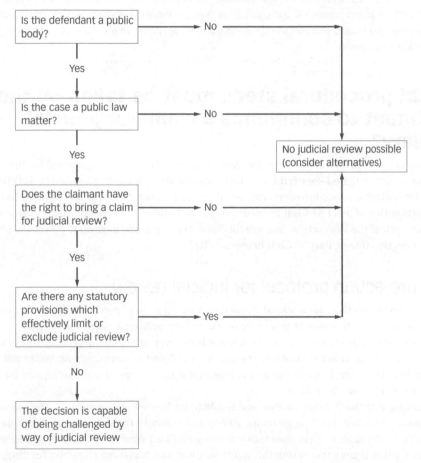

Figure 11.1

Is judicial review inappropriate on policy grounds?

Judicial review is discretionary. Even if the defendant is a public body, the matter is within public law, the claimant has the right to claim, and Parliament has not excluded judicial review the High Court may refuse to exercise the supervisory jurisdiction if it is thought inappropriate to do so. This is a question of policy.

....

R v Cambridge Health Authority, ex p B [1995] 1 WLR 898

The Court of Appeal considered whether it was appropriate to review and quash the decision of a health authority to refuse to fund treatment where it was revolutionary and chances of success were limited or unknown. It was held that the health authority's decision was not unlawful. It would be inappropriate for the court to review the funding priorities of such bodies where resources are limited and budgeting necessary or to intervene where matters of medical judgment are concerned.

....

What procedural steps must be taken by the claimant to commence a claim for judicial review?

The law is contained in the **s 31 of the Senior Courts Act 1981** as amended by the **Civil Procedure Act 1997** and the **Civil Procedure (Modification of the Senior Courts Act) Order 2004**. The detailed procedure is contained in the **Pre-Action Protocol for Judicial Review** and **Section One of Part 54 Civil Procedural Rules**. Judicial review procedure begins with consideration of the Pre-Action Protocol for Judicial Review and goes on to follow the provisions of **Section One of Part 54 Civil Procedure Rules**.

The pre-action protocol for judicial review

The **Pre-Action Protocol for Judicial Review** provides a code of good practice and contains the steps which parties should generally follow before making a claim for judicial review. There are some types of cases in which it is not necessary to follow the procedural requirements of the **Pre-Action Protocol** and the claimant is free to determine whether or not it is appropriate. However, if the claimant decides that it is not appropriate the reason for this must be stated in the claim form.

Assuming that the **Pre-Action Protocol for Judicial Review** is appropriate, the following procedural steps remain. The claimant writes and sends to the defendant a letter before claim. The defendant is given fourteen days to write and send to the claimant a letter in response. If the claimant is acting through a solicitor, and is relying on public funding, this is the appropriate time for the solicitor to advise on and organize funding.

Initial procedure under Part 54 of the Civil Procedure Rules (section One)

Section One of **Part 54 Civil Procedure Rules** must be used where the claimant claims a quashing order, mandatory order, or prohibiting order. **Section One** may be used where the claimant seeks a declaration or an injunction. The claimant must ask for permission to proceed with a claim for judicial review. Among other things, the claim form requires the claimant to specify the decision being challenged; the date the decision was made; the date on which the claimant became aware of the decision; the factual background to the claim; the grounds upon which the claimant challenges the decision; the remedies being sought; and whether the case raises any issues under the **Human Rights Act 1998**.

The claimant, or their solicitor, makes a Statement of Truth and must prepare a bundle of supporting documents. The claim has to be made to the Administrative Court promptly and in any event not later than three months after the grounds to make the claim first arose. The claimant must serve a copy of the claim form on the defendant and any other person the claimant considers to be an interested party within seven days after the date of issue.

Appeals

An appeal lies with permission from the decision of the Administrative Court to the Court of Appeal.

Remedies and judicial review

Revision tip

You do not have to spend too much time revising remedies. The most important things to remember are that all remedies in judicial review are discretionary and that there are some remedies which are available only by judicial review. You also need to appreciate what each remedy achieves and your reason for choosing it.

The following remedies may be claimed only by judicial review:

Quashing order

The court examines the defendant public authority's proceedings. If there is any illegality, irrationality, or procedural impropriety its decision is empty of legal effect.

Mandatory order

This is an order to do something as the law requires.

Prohibiting order

This is an order not to do something or to discontinue doing something which is unlawful.

The following remedies may be claimed by judicial review procedure:

Key cases

An injunction

These may be mandatory or prohibitive.

A declaration

This is a statement declaring whether something the defendant public authority has done or is about to do is unlawful. **Section 4 Human Rights Act 1998** gives the High Court in England and Wales the jurisdiction to state whether a statute is compatible with Convention rights.

Damages in conjunction with any other remedy available by judicial review

Part 54 Civil Procedure Rules provides that a claim for judicial review may include a claim for damages, restitution, or the recovery of a sum due but a claimant may not seek such a remedy alone.

 **Key cases**

Case	Facts	Principle
Clark v University of Lincolnshire and Humberside [2000] 3 All ER 752	The Court of Appeal had to decide whether the claimant had abused the process of the court by claiming that the university was in breach of contract in the way it had applied its own student regulations.	It is not an abuse of process for a student at a university where there is no charter or appointed visitor to claim breach of contract by private law procedure.
O'Reilly v Mackman [1982] 3 All ER 1124	The House of Lords had to decide whether the claimants had abused the process of the court by bringing their claim under private law procedure.	As a general rule it would be contrary to public policy and an abuse of the process of the court for a claimant complaining of a public authority's infringement of his public law rights to seek redress by ordinary action.
R v Cambridge Health Authority, ex p B [1995] 2 All ER 129	The Court of Appeal had to decide whether it was appropriate to review the decision of a health authority which had refused to fund treatment.	Unless a public authority exceeds or abuses its powers, it is not appropriate for the court to intervene especially where matters of professional judgement are concerned. It is also not appropriate for the court to pass judgment on the way a public authority, acting within its powers, spends its allocated budget.
R v Disciplinary Committee of the Jockey Club, ex p Aga Khan [1993] 1 WLR 909	The Court of Appeal had to decide whether the Disciplinary Committee of the Jockey Club was amenable to judicial review.	Such a body will not be amenable to judicial review unless it is clear that its origin, history, constitution, and membership show that it has been woven into a system of governmental control.

Case	Facts	Principle
R v Panel on Take-overs and Mergers, ex p Datafin [1987] QB 815	The Court of Appeal had to decide whether the Code of Practice Committee of the city panel on takeovers and mergers was susceptible to judicial review.	A non-statutory self-regulatory body may be amenable to judicial review if there is a sufficient public element in its functions.

⑨⑨ Key debates

Topic	*R (on the application of Mullins) v Jockey Club Appeal Board (No 1)* [2005] EWHC 2197; Times, 24 October 2005 (QBD (Admin))
Author/ Academic	Case Report
Viewpoint	Considers the claimant's contention that the Court of Appeal decision in *R v Disciplinary Committee of the Jockey Club, ex p The Aga Khan* (1993) could be distinguished from the present case on various grounds. The article also considers academic criticisms of *ex p Aga Khan*.
Source	(2006) 1(Feb) International Sports Law Review 30–38.

Topic	'Public Law Procedures and Remedies – Do we Need Them?'
Author/ Academic	Dawn Oliver
Viewpoint	Considers whether orders of certiorari, mandamus, and prohibition should be retained as remedies available on judicial review and whether special procedural rules governing judicial review are still necessary.
Source	[2002] PL 91–110.

Topic	'*Clark*: The Demise of *O'Reilly* Completed?'
Author/ Academic	Tom Hickman
Viewpoint	Case law illustrating the shift away from strict rule of procedural exclusivity laid down in *O'Reilly v Mackman* (1983), focusing on implications of ruling in *Clark* (2000) on the effect of the **Civil Procedure Rules** on the distinction between public and private law.
Source	(2000) 5(3) Judicial Review, 178–183.

Exam questions

Topic	'Functions of a Public Nature under the Human Rights Act'
Author/ Academic	Dawn Oliver
Viewpoint	Considers the scope of **s 6(3)(b) Human Rights Act 1998**, which allows judicial review of 'functions of a public nature' if exercised incompatibly with the European Convention on Human Rights.
Source	[2004] PL 329–351.

Topic	'The Question of What Constitutes a Public Body for the Purposes of Judicial Review'
Author/ Academic	Michael J Beloff
Viewpoint	This article reviews the Jockey Club cases and addresses the current debate concerning the reviewability of sports organizations. It examines the options open to the House of Lords if it ever has to decide whether such bodies should be open to judicial review.
Source	[2006] 1(Feb) International Sports Law Review 1–3.

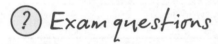 (?) Exam questions

Problem question

Antonio makes and sells ice cream. The Food Standards Authority is a non-statutory body which lays down rules concerning the quality and safety of food. All manufacturers and retailers must comply with the rules laid down by the Food Standards Authority. It has power to discipline and ultimately ban any manufacturer or retailer who makes or sells food which does not comply with the rules.

Antonio is accused of making and selling poor quality ice cream which is believed to have been responsible for an outbreak of food poisoning. Antonio is subsequently banned from making and selling ice cream by the Food Standards Authority. Both he and the Society of Ice Cream Manufacturers are unhappy about the decision and seek your advice.

Advise Antonio and the Society of Ice Cream Manufacturers as to whether, and if so on what basis, the Food Standards Authority is a public body, capable of being subject to judicial review.

Advise Antonio and the Society of Ice Cream Manufacturers as to whether the decision of the Food Standards Authority is a public law matter.

Advise the Society of Ice Cream Manufacturers as to whether it would have the right to challenge the decision either on its own behalf or on Antonio's behalf.

Advise Antonio and the Society of Ice Cream Manufacturers as to the procedure they would be expected to follow should they decide to apply for judicial review and the remedies they would seek.

Outline answers are included at the end of the book.

Essay question

Explain what is meant by public law and the extent to which, if at all, the distinction between public and private law is important when deciding if judicial review is appropriate.

 Scan here

Scan this QR code image with your mobile device to see an outline answer to this question or log onto www.oxfordtextbooks.co.uk/orc/concentrate

#12

Grounds for judicial review

Key Facts

- Judicial review is based on technical grounds.

- These are classified as illegality, irrationality, and procedural impropriety.

- Illegality includes *ultra vires*, improper purpose, irrelevant considerations, lack of evidence, and unlawfully failing to exercise a discretionary power.

- Irrationality means unreasonableness which is now linked to the principle of proportionality.

- Procedural impropriety focuses on natural justice and failure to observe procedural rules.

- A fair hearing includes the right to be heard, adequate notice, and the right to answer the allegations made.

- Everyone is entitled to an unbiased hearing.

- Although there is no general duty to give reasons for a decision in English law there are significant exceptions to this rule.

The classification of grounds for judicial review

Lord Diplock, in *Council of Civil Service Unions v Minister for the Civil Service* (1985) classified the grounds for judicial review as: **illegality**, irrationality, and **procedural impropriety**.

Illegality

Illegality includes *ultra vires*, improper purpose, relevant and irrelevant considerations, lack of evidence, and failure to exercise a discretionary power.

Ultra vires

A public body must not go beyond its powers. This is the *ultra vires* doctrine. The court has to decide whether a public body has the power to do something. The matters the court is entitled to take into account when doing this were determined by the Court of Appeal in the following case.

....

White and Collins v Minister of Health [1939] 2 KB 838

The **Housing Act 1936** provided that local authorities could compulsorily purchase land for the purpose of slum clearance. Parks, gardens, and pleasure grounds were exempt. Any slum clearance scheme had to be approved by the Minister of Health. The Court of Appeal had to decide whether it had jurisdiction to consider whether a piece of land formed part of a park, garden, or pleasure ground within the meaning of the **1936 Act** after the Minister of Health had decided to confirm a compulsory purchase order for the purposes of slum clearance.

The key principle is that a court which has to consider whether a public body has acted within its powers must be entitled to review all the vital findings on which the existence of the power depends, including findings of fact. That jurisdiction is not reduced by ministerial confirmation of a local authority's decision.

Illegality
✳✳✳✳✳✳✳✳✳✳✳✳

It was held that the decision to make a compulsory purchase order was *ultra vires* because the land in question was part of a park and was, therefore, exempt under the provisions of the **Housing Act 1936**.

In the case of a statutory power, the court is entitled to interpret the words of the statute. The established rules and presumptions of statutory interpretation are used for this purpose. The court then decides whether or not the action or decision lies inside or outside the power the statute confers.

In *Attorney General v Fulham Corporation* (1921) Sargant J held that Fulham Corporation had the power, under the **Baths and Wash Houses Acts 1846 and 1847**, to provide public baths and self-service facilities for the washing of clothes. It did not have the power to set up a municipal laundry.

Jurisdictional error

Revision tip

You should spend more time revising this topic. It illustrates how the *ultra vires* doctrine has been widened.

Although many judicial review cases are concerned with whether a public body has the power to make a decision, many others are concerned with whether a public body has misinterpreted or abused its powers. The distinction between jurisdictional and non-jurisdictional error is important.

A **jurisdictional error** is a mistake of law amounting to illegality, irrationality, or procedural impropriety within a public body's decision-making process. When it makes such an error a public body acts outside its jurisdiction. Jurisdiction, in this context, means the power to inquire or decide.

A **non-jurisdictional** error does not take a public body outside its jurisdiction. It may be reversible on appeal but only if there is a right to do so. If there is no right of appeal the error may be unchallengeable.

The *ultra vires* doctrine has been widened so that any misinterpretation or abuse of power made by a public body is capable of being a jurisdictional error. A public body may misinterpret or abuse its powers if it acts in bad faith; or fails to comply with the rules of natural justice; or misinterprets its powers so that it takes into account something it had no power to consider or fails to take into account any relevant matters; or does anything capable of being a ground for judicial review.

This was determined by the House of Lords in the following case.

Anisminic v Foreign Compensation Commission [1969] 2 AC 147

Following the 1956 Suez Crisis, property owned by Anisminic (Ac) was nationalized by the Egyptian Government and given to an Egyptian organization called TEDO. Anisminic negotiated a financial settlement with the Egyptian Government. Subsequently, the British Government nego-tiated a treaty with the Egyptian Government. Under its terms, funds were set aside to com-pensate British nationals. The Foreign Compensation Commission (FCC), empowered by the **Foreign Compensation Act 1950**, was given the job of determining entitlement to compensa-tion. Anisminic's claim was rejected by the FCC on the ground that it had 'sold' its property to TEDO which was Anisminic's successor in title but not a British national. Anisminic claimed a declaration from the High Court that the FCC's decision was null and void. The case reached the House of Lords.

The key principle is that the word 'determination' in the Act should not be construed as includ-ing everything which purported to be a determination because the commission had misconstrued the statutory regulations defining their jurisdiction.

The House of Lords granted the declaration. It was held that the FCC had made a jurisdictional error and had misunderstood the meaning of 'successor in title'. TEDO was not a successor in title so that the FCC had no jurisdiction to consider TEDO's nationality.

Revision tip

Although **Anisminic** is primarily concerned with jurisdiction, it links up with all the technical bases for the grounds for judicial review considered in this chapter. When you revise grounds for judicial review, you should remember that the court is concerned as much with how a public body exercises the powers it has as it is with whether it had the power to do something.

✔ Looking for extra marks?

You should read the dissenting speeches, compare and contrast them, and then compare them with the majority speeches.

In *R v Lord President of the Privy Council, ex p Page* (1993) Lord Browne-Wilkinson said that the decision in *Anisminic Ltd v Foreign Compensation Commission* (1969) rendered obsolete the distinction between non-jurisdictional errors and other errors of law by extend-ing the doctrine of *ultra vires*. Lord Griffiths said that public bodies must apply the law cor-rectly. If they make an error of law during the decision-making process the decision can be quashed by judicial review.

The Supreme Court in *R (Cart) v Upper Tribunal* (2011) had to decide whether the desig-nation of the Upper Tribunal as a 'superior court of record' by s 3 of the **Tribunals, Courts and Enforcement Act 2007** meant that its decisions were not amenable to the supervisory jurisdiction of the High Court. The key principle is that the words used by the 2007 Act are not clear enough to exclude judicial review of unappealable decisions of the Upper Tribunal. Parliament never intends to perpetuate errors of law. There should be the possibility that a second judge, who should always be someone with more experience or expertise than the judge who first heard the case, could check for errors in the case. In order to keep important errors to a minimum and to provide the level of independent scrutiny outside the tribunal structure required by the rule of law, while recognizing that the enhanced tribunal set up under the 2007 Act deserved a restrained approach to judicial review and that the best use should be made of the courts' limited judicial resources, the criteria upon which permission to make a second-tier appeal to the Court of Appeal was granted should be adopted in relation to applications for permission to proceed with claims for judicial review.

Revision Tip

See chapter 11. In a problem question you may be asked to discuss whether a public body has the power to make a decision. If so refer to the empowering statute to determine the nature and extent of the power which is conferred.

The ultra vires doctrine and subjective discretionary powers

Statutes sometimes say that a public body *may* do something. This is a discretionary power. When a public body considers a claim, it may decide how it will exercise the power: It may act, with or without conditions, or refuse to act. Statutes sometimes provide that a power may be exercised as a public body sees fit or if the Secretary of State is satisfied or if they reasonably believe it is necessary. This is a subjective discretion. In times of war or emergency the courts often refuse to intervene on the basis that, subject to the requirement of good faith, the executive is better placed than the judiciary to make a decision. This was the case in the House of Lords' decisions in *Liversidge v Anderson* (1942) and *Secretary of State for the Home Department v Rehman* (2003). See chapter 3.

In other contexts the court may be prepared to imply words into statutes and make a discretionary power subject to implied principles, undertakings, and duties. Examples of this are social policy, local government finance, and the relationship between local and central government. One implied duty the courts impose is that if a public body is given powers to spend public money it owes a duty to taxpayers to use the money in a businesslike manner with reasonable skill and caution. Political promises do not create legally binding obligations.

....

Bromley London Borough Council v Greater London Council [1983] 1 AC 768

The Greater London Council (GLC) resolved that the London Boroughs should contribute 6.1p in the pound towards reducing bus and tube fares by 25%. The London Borough of Bromley applied for judicial review.

The key principle is that public bodies generally and local authorities in particular owe a duty to taxpayers to have regard to the interests of taxpayers when making decisions involving public spending. Wide discretionary powers are impliedly limited. These limitations depend upon the structure and status of the body. The House of Lords held that the GLC's discretionary powers were impliedly limited by an obligation to run London Transport Services in a businesslike way and that they were in breach of that implied obligation. They were also in breach of their duty to taxpayers. The proposed scheme was *ultra vires*.

....

Improper purpose

A public body must exercise a discretionary power for the purpose for which it is granted. If a statute states the purposes for which discretion is to be exercised, the courts will treat the stated purposes as exhaustive. If the discretion is exercised for a different purpose, the decision will be invalid. This is illustrated by the Court of Appeal decision in the following case.

....

Congreve v Home Office [1976] QB 629

The claimant renewed his television licence early to avoid an increase in the TV licence fee. His TV licence was revoked. The Home Secretary said that he was entitled to revoke TV licences under **s 1(4)** of the **Wireless Telegraphy Act 1949**. The claimant sought a declaration that the revocation of his TV licence was unlawful.

The key principle is that a statutory power conferred on a minister for the purpose of granting and revoking licences cannot be used for the unauthorized purpose of raising money.

The Court of Appeal granted a declaration.

....

If the statute does not specify the purposes for which discretion may be exercised, the court can impose implied restrictions. Statutory powers may not be used so as to defeat the policy and purpose of the Act (determined by the House of Lords in *Padfield v Minister of Agriculture* (1968)); penalize conduct (held in *R v Lewisham LBC, ex p Shell UK Ltd* (1988)); promote the political or moral views of the decision maker (see *R v Secretary of State for Foreign Affairs, ex p World Development Movement* (1996)); or gain an unauthorized financial advantage (laid down by the Court of Appeal in *Hall v Shoreham UDC* (1964)).

Mixed motives

A public body may do something for more than one reason. Some may be valid while others are not. The court adopts one of two approaches. It may look for the dominant or true purpose and if that is authorized the court will hold that the decision is lawful even though some secondary or incidental purposes are technically outside the public body's powers as determined by the House of Lords in *Westminster Corporation v London & Northwestern Railway Co* (1905). Alternatively the court may distinguish between the primary and secondary purpose and if the secondary purpose has significantly influenced the decision-making process the decision will be invalid as laid down in *R v ILEA, ex p Inner London Education Authority* (1986).

Relevant and irrelevant considerations

A public body must take into account relevant matters and discard anything irrelevant. Where the relevant considerations are expressly stated in a statute any deviation will make a decision invalid. This was the key principle in **R v Secretary of State for the Home Department, ex p Venables and Thompson (1998).** Here the House of Lords decided to quash the Home Secretary's decision because he had taken into account public opinion and his own policies and had not considered the welfare of the applicants as required by **s 44(1)** of the **Children and Young Persons Act 1933**.

If the statute does not specifically instruct the public body concerning relevant considerations, the court adopts a similar approach to improper purpose. This is illustrated by cases such as *R v Lewisham LBC, ex p Shell* (1988) and *R v Somerset County Council, ex p Fewings* (1995) where the improper purposes could also be classified as irrelevant considerations. It also links up to cases like *Bromley v GLC* (1983) and *Padfield v Minister of Agriculture* (1968).

Lack of evidence

This is based on the Court of Appeal decision in *Coleen Properties v Minister of Housing and Local Government* (1971). The key principle is that a public body must base its conclusions of fact on the evidence before it. It cannot make a decision which differs from the findings of fact put before it unless there is evidence to support a contrary conclusion.

Unlawful failure to exercise a discretionary power

This ground for judicial review was explained by Lord Reid in the House of Lords' decision in *British Oxygen Co Ltd v Minster of Technology* (1971). Lord Reid said that there are two general grounds on which the exercise of an unqualified discretion can be attacked. It must not be exercised in bad faith, and it must not be so unreasonably exercised as to show that there cannot have been any real or genuine exercise of the discretion. But, apart from that, if the minister thinks that policy or good administration requires the operation of some limiting rule, there is nothing to stop him.

Lord Reid went on to say that the general rule is that anyone who has to exercise a statutory discretion must not shut his ears to an application. There is no great difference between a policy and a rule. There may be cases where an officer or authority ought to listen to a substantial argument, reasonably presented, urging a change of policy. What the authority must not do is to refuse to listen at all.

A public body cannot limit its discretion by unlawfully refusing to exercise its jurisdiction by adopting a policy which shuts its ears to certain types of application. This principle was applied by the House of Lords in *R v Secretary of State for the Home Department, ex p Hindley* (2001). This case concerned the discretionary power of the Home Secretary to release mandatory life sentence prisoners under **s 27** of the **Prison Act 1952**. The Home Secretary had adopted a policy that a review and reduction of a sentence would be considered only in exceptional circumstances including exceptional progress. It was alleged that he had unlawfully fettered his discretion. The House of Lords held that the Home Secretary had not unlawfully fettered his discretion because his policy did not rule out reconsideration from time to time. A public body cannot limit its discretion unlawfully by estoppels based on a representation made by an official that the claimant had the right to do something (held in *Western Fish Products v Penrith DC* (1981)); an agreement (see *Stringer v Minister of Housing* (1971); or wrongful delegation (as in *Barnard v National Dock Labour Board* (1953)).

Irrationality

In Lord Diplock's scheme, irrationality means **unreasonableness**.

The House of Lords, in *Roberts v Hopwood* (1925), determined that discretionary powers must be exercised reasonably. Lord Greene MR in *Associated Provincial Picture Houses Ltd v Wednesbury Corporation* (1948) said that unreasonableness is a comprehensively used term capable of meaning that a person given a discretionary power has not directed himself properly in law; has acted in bad faith; failed to pay attention to all the matters he is bound to consider; based his decision on irrelevant considerations; or reached a conclusion which is so absurd that no reasonable authority could ever have come to it.

It is very difficult to prove that a decision is so absurd that no reasonable authority could ever have come to it. This requires something overwhelming. In *Backhouse v Lambeth LBC* (1972) a housing authority passed a resolution under the **Housing Act 1957 s 111(1)** increasing the rent of an unoccupied and unfit house by £18,000 a week. It did this in order to be able to invoke the provisions of the **Housing Finance Act 1972 s 63 (1)** exempting it from increasing rents of council houses under **s 62**. The resolution was one which no reasonable authority could have passed and was accordingly a nullity.

Irrationality in the context of human rights was considered by the Court of Appeal in the following case.

....

R v Ministry of Defence, ex p Smith [1996] QB 517

By a statement made in 1994 the Ministry of Defence reaffirmed its policy that homosexuality was incompatible with service in the armed forces and that personnel known to be homosexual or engaging in homosexual activity would be administratively discharged. The four applicants were serving members of the armed forces who had been administratively discharged between November 1994 and January 1995 on the sole ground that they were of homosexual orientation. In proceedings for judicial review each applicant challenged the decision. One of the grounds was irrationality.

The key principle is that where an administrative decision is made in the context of human rights the court will require a proportionately greater justification before being satisfied that the decision is within the range of responses open to a reasonable decision-maker, according to the seriousness of the interference with those rights. Applying the test of irrationality, which is sufficiently flexible to cover all situations, the court will show greater caution where the nature of the decision is esoteric, policy-laden, or security-based.

The Court of Appeal decided that the policy was not irrational.

....

Proportionality

Proportionality means that there must be a reasonable relationship between the objective being sought and the means used to achieve it. The possibility that proportionality might become an independent ground for judicial review was first discussed by Lord Diplock in *Council of Civil Service Unions v Minister for the Civil Service* (1985). There was also speculation about how the principle would develop by Lord Roskill and Lord Bridge in *R v Secretary of State for the Home Department, ex p Brind* (1991). But these cases were inconclusive. Lord Slynn, however, in *R (Alconbury Developments Ltd) v Secretary of State for the Environment, Transport and the Regions* (2003) said that it is time to recognize proportionality as a principle of English administrative law. This principle is applied in cases where the court is asked to consider whether legislation is compatible with Convention rights; applying principles of European Union law; deciding whether to quash a penalty or punishment; asked to review the decision of a public body on the ground that it is unreasonable.

The distinction between merits-based and procedural review

The basic difference between an appeal and judicial review is explained in chapter 10.

In *Associated Provincial Picture Houses Ltd v Wednesbury Corporation* (1948) Lord Greene MR made it clear that the courts can interfere with executive decisions only if it is shown that a public body has contravened the law. The court, when exercising its supervisory jurisdiction, is not a court of appeal. It must not substitute its own opinion for that of the authority. When discretion is granted the law recognizes certain principles upon which that discretion must be exercised, but within those principles the discretion is absolute and cannot be questioned in any court. Lord Ackner, in *R v Secretary of State for the Home Department, ex p Brind* (1991), said that it would be wrong for the judiciary to quash an executive decision on its merits. It would invite an abuse of power by the judiciary. The test of *Wednesbury* unreasonableness was necessarily severe to confine the jurisdiction exercised by the judiciary to a supervisory, as opposed to an appellate, jurisdiction.

Section 2 of the **Human Rights Act 1998 Act** obliges the courts to take into account the principles formulated and applied by the European Court of Human Rights including proportionality, which, according to Lord Slynn in the *Alconbury Case,* cannot exist in a separate compartment from **Wednesbury** unreasonableness. Moreover, Laws LJ in *R (Mahmood) v Secretary of State for the Home Department* (2001) said that it is a recognized common law principle that the intensity of review in a public law case will depend on the subject matter in hand. Any interference by the action of a public body with a fundamental right will require a substantial objective justification. This was accepted and discussed by Lord Steyn in the House of Lords' decision in *R (Daly) v Secretary of State for the Home Department* (2001). He said that the court must look at how the decision-maker strikes a balance with fundamental rights. Proportionality may go further than the traditional grounds of review. The intensity of the review, in similar cases, is guaranteed by the twin requirements that the limitation of the right was necessary in a democratic society, in the sense of meeting a pressing social need, and the question whether the interference was really proportionate to the legitimate aim being pursued. He would not go as far to say that there had been a shift to merits-based review. Again, in the *Alconbury Case* Lord Slynn said that there was nothing in Strasbourg jurisprudence to suggest a merits-based approach to judicial review.

✅ *Looking for extra marks?*

Proportionality, irrationality, and the distinction between merits-based and procedural review have been the subjects of intense academic debate. You should look up and read the following articles and materials to gain a fuller understanding. These are set out in the key debates feature at the end of this chapter. see in particular:

Professor Jeffrey Jowell QC, 'Beyond the Rule of Law: Towards Constitutional Judicial Review' [2000] PL 671, and

Professor David Feldman, 'Proportionality and the Human Rights Act 1998', essay in *The Principle of Proportionality in the Laws of Europe* edited by Evelyn Ellis (1999), pp 117, 127 *et seq.*

Procedural impropriety

This means breach of the rules of natural justice and failure to comply with statutory procedural requirements.

Revision tip

When considering procedural impropriety, you should consider if the rules of natural justice apply in principle and then the extent to which they apply to the body concerned.

The rules of natural justice are that no man is to be a judge in his own cause and the parties to a dispute shall be fairly heard.

Do the rules of natural justice apply in principle?

The rules of natural justice apply to all judicial proceedings. For a long time there was a strict distinction between judicial and administrative bodies. The rules of natural justice applied to judicial bodies. They did not apply to authorities exercising purely administrative functions. That changed with the House of Lords' decision in *Ridge v Baldwin* (1964). Lord Reid held that the rules of natural justice are capable of applying in principle where an administrative body acts judicially. He went on to say that 'judicial' meant any decision affecting the rights of the individual.

To what extent do the rules of natural justice apply?

Lord Bridge, in the House of Lords' decision in *Lloyd v McMahon* (1987), said that the requirements of natural justice depend, among other things, on the circumstances of the case; the nature of the inquiry; the rules under which the tribunal is acting; and the subject matter.

Licensing

A licence gives a person permission to do something, which might otherwise constitute a criminal offence. Statute empowers bodies to act as licensing authorities and enables them to issue, renew, and revoke licences. The statutes will also lay down rules, conditions, and procedural requirements which the licensing authority has to follow. As to whether, and to what extent, such bodies are bound by the rules of natural justice depends upon the type of matter being considered.

There are three recognized categories of licensing case, namely application cases, expectation cases, and revocation cases.

An application case concerns someone who merely seeks to obtain a licence when they do not already have one. In an expectation case the claimant says that he legitimately expects that a licence will be granted. Such an expectation is usually based on past experience. This may occur where the applicant applies for renewal of a licence. A revocation case is one in which the licensing authority seeks to take away some existing right or position. In all three categories, the rules of natural justice apply in principle but to differing extents. In application cases, for instance, there is a basic duty to consider applications fairly and on their merits but nothing more. The rules apply more rigorously to expectation and revocation cases. These rules were laid down by Megarry VC in the following case.

McInnes v Onslow Fane [1978] 3 All ER 211

The claimant applied to the British Boxing Board of Control (the Board) for a boxers' manager's licence. He also asked for an oral hearing and prior information of anything that might militate against a favourable recommendation. The Board refused his application. He was given neither an oral hearing, nor reasons for the refusal. The claimant applied for a declaration that the Board was in breach of the rules of natural justice.

It was held that although the Board was subject to the rules of natural justice, as an applicant, the claimant was only entitled to expect that the Board would reach an honest conclusion without bias or caprice. The Board was not under any obligation to provide an oral hearing. The declaration was refused.

An application case

In *R v Gaming Board, ex p Beniam and Khaida* (1970), the Court of Appeal said that although the Gaming Board must act fairly it is not obliged to disclose sources or details of information or their reasons when refusing a certificate of consent.

An expectation case

In *R v Liverpool CC, ex p Liverpool Taxi Fleet Operators' Association* (1975) a taxicab licensing authority gave a public undertaking not to increase the number of licences. This created a legitimate expectation and gave the court grounds to intervene.

A revocation case

In *R v Barnsley MBC, ex p Hook* (1976) the key principle is that a local authority reviewing a decision to revoke the licence of a market trader to operate from a stall on a market controlled by the authority has a duty to act judicially and in accordance with the rules of natural justice.

Have the rules of natural justice been breached?

Bias

Revision tip

When you come to this part of your answer you need to break it down to consider first, whether there is pecuniary or personal bias and, secondly, whether there is a real possibility or real danger of bias.

No man shall be a judge in his own cause. Both sides in a dispute have the right to expect that the matter will be impartially adjudicated. There are two types of bias. The first is pecuniary bias. The second is personal bias. Pecuniary bias arises where the adjudicator may have a financial interest in the outcome of a decision. In *Dimes v Grand Junction Canal* (1852) the Lord Chancellor was held to be disqualified from hearing a case because he was a shareholder in the company which was a party to the action. Personal bias is anything which might cause an adjudicator to view one side in a dispute more or less favourably than the other. In *Bradford v McLeod* (1986) a Scottish judge said, at a social function during a miners' strike, that he would not grant legal aid to miners. Subsequently a miner represented by a solicitor who had heard the sheriff's remarks appeared for trial before the same sheriff on a summary complaint alleging breach of the peace at a picket line. The solicitor asked the sheriff to disqualify himself. The sheriff refused. It was held that the sheriff should have disqualified himself because a reasonable person would see a danger of personal bias.

The rule that it is not enough that justice should be done but that justice must also be seen to be done goes back to Lord Hewart CJ's decision in *R v Sussex Justices, ex p McCarthy* (1924). This means that the party alleging bias does not have to prove that the adjudicator *was* biased. In the House of Lords' decision in *R v Gough* (1993) Lord Goff held that the party alleging bias had to prove that there was a real danger of bias. The test was modified by the House of Lords in the following case:

....

Porter v Magill [2002] 2 AC 357

This case involved many issues including the question of whether the test concerning bias formulated by Lord Goff in *R v Gough* (1993) and subsequent cases needed to be modified.

The key principle is that when considering bias the court will ascertain all the circumstances which have a bearing on the suggestion that the judge was biased and ask whether those circumstances would lead a fair minded and informed observer to conclude that there was a real possibility or a real danger that the tribunal was biased. There is no difference in meaning between real possibility and real danger.

On this issue, the law was modified.

. . . .

The right to be fairly heard

Revision tip

This is the heart of the subject. Revise it thoroughly. This also has important human rights implications. You should link this up with your revision of the material contained in chapter 14.

Both sides in a dispute have the right to be heard. Lord Hodson, in *Ridge v Baldwin* **(1964)** said that there were three outstanding features of a fair hearing the right to be heard by an unbiased tribunal; the right to have notice of charges of misconduct; and the right to be heard in answer to those charges.

. . . .

Ridge v Baldwin [1964] AC 40

A Chief Constable was dismissed for being negligent in the discharge of his duty under **s 191** of the **Municipal Corporations Act 1882**. The committee which dismissed him did not say how he was negligent and the initial decision was taken in his absence. The appellant then brought an action against members of the committee for a declaration that his dismissal was illegal, *ultra vires*, and void, and payment of salary from 7 March 1958, or, alternatively, payment of pension from that date and damages. The declaration was granted by the House of Lords.

. . . .

A party to the proceedings must be given the opportunity to state his case and to challenge and correct anything that is presented to a decision-maker that might be prejudicial to his case. For example in *Errington v Minister of Health* **(1935)** it was determined that when a minister conducts an inquiry he is performing a judicial function and must invite objectors to the meeting and hear their objections before making a final decision.

In *R v Thames Magistrates' Court, ex p Polemis* **(1974)** the claimant was the master of a ship who was convicted by magistrates of an offence in his absence because the summons was issued on the day his ship was due to sail and an adjournment was refused. It was held that the applicant had been deprived of the opportunity to present his case in that he had been given no reasonable opportunity to prepare his case before the hearing, and in those circumstances there had been a denial of natural justice.

The right to legal representation is mandatory in any court or tribunal. In other contexts the right is discretionary and depends upon the seriousness of the charge and of the penalty; the likelihood of points of law arising; the ability of the party to conduct his case; and the need for speed in making an adjudication. This was determined in *R v Secretary of State for the Home Department, ex p Tarrant* **(1985)**.

The right to be given reasons for a decision

There is no general obligation to give reasons for a decision in English law. There are, however, significant exceptions.

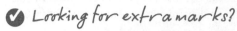 **Looking for extra marks?**

Lord Bingham CJ, in *R v Ministry of Defence, ex p Murray* (1998), gave detailed guidance on the principles to be applied when deciding whether or not to give reasons for a decision. You should look this case up and read the principles.

Lord Mustill in *R v Secretary of State for the Home Department, ex p Doody (1994)* said that the principles of fairness are not to be applied by rote identically in every situation. What fairness demands is dependent on the context of the decision. Lord Mustill went on to say that the giving of reasons may be inconvenient, but he could see no ground at all why it should be against the public interest.

Legitimate expectation

A person may have a legitimate expectation of being treated in a certain way by an administrative authority even though there is no other legal basis upon which he could claim such treatment.

A legitimate expectation may arise from a representation or promise; a consistent past practice, and the conduct of the decision-maker. The basic principle is that the principles of fairness, predictability, and certainty should not be disregarded, provided there are no overriding policy considerations like national security.

Council of Civil Service Unions v Minister for the Civil Service [1985] AC 374

The claimants sought judicial review of a decision of the Minister for the Civil Service (the Prime Minister) to ban trade union membership at a defence establishment on national security grounds.

The key principle here is that a legitimate expectation may arise based on consistent past practice.

It was held that the applicants would, apart from considerations of national security, have had a legitimate expectation that unions and employees would be consulted before the minister issued her instruction of 22 December 1983, and, accordingly, the decision-making process would have been unfair by reason of her failure to consult them and would have been amenable to judicial review.

An example of legitimate expectation based on promises can be seen in the Court of Appeal decision in the following case.

Key cases

R v North and East Devon Health Body, ex p Coughlan [2001] QB 213

The key principle is that if a public body exercising a statutory function makes a promise as to how it will behave in the future which induces a legitimate expectation of a benefit which is substantive, rather than merely procedural, to frustrate that expectation can be so unfair that it will amount to an abuse of power. In such circumstances, the court had to determine whether there was a sufficient overriding interest to justify a departure from what had previously been promised.

These principles were reviewed by the House of Lords in the following case.

R (Bancoult) v Secretary of State for Foreign and Commonwealth Affairs (No 2) [2009] 1 AC 453

The House of Lords had to decide whether a statement made by the Secretary of State revoking immigration controls in 2000 created a legitimate expectation that the Changos Islanders would be allowed to return and settle permanently on the outer islands.

The key principle applied here is that legitimate expectation has to be based on a promise which is both clear and unambiguous.

The House of Lords decided that no legitimate expectation had been created on which the islanders could rely.

 Key cases

Case	Facts	Principle
Associated Provincial Picture Houses Ltd v Wednesbury Corporation [1948] 1 KB 223	The Court of Appeal had to decide whether conditions attached to the licensing of cinemas for Sunday opening were reasonable.	For a decision to be unreasonable it must so absurd that no sensible person could ever contemplate that it would be within their decision-making powers.
Bromley London Borough Council v Greater London Council [1983] 1 AC 768	The House of Lords had to decide whether the Greater London Council was within its powers to require the London Boroughs to contribute financially to a scheme to reduce London Transport fares by 25%.	The discretionary powers of the Greater London Council were limited by implied fiduciary duties and undertakings to run London Transport on business principles.

Case	Facts	Principle
Council of Civil Service Unions v Minister for the Civil Service [1985] AC 374	The Civil Service Union challenged a decision to ban trade union membership at GCHQ on national security grounds.	In the absence of overriding national security considerations a legitimate expectation of consultation was capable of arising based on consistent past practice.
Porter v Magill [2002] 2 AC 357	This concerned an appeal following an allegation of misconduct within Westminster City Council.	The test to be applied for determining the existence of apparent bias was whether a fair minded and informed observer would conclude that there was a real possibility of bias. Applying such test, P's claim was unsubstantiated and, in view of the nature of the investigation, the delay was not unreasonable.
Ridge v Baldwin [1964] AC 40	Under s 191 Municipal Corporations Act 1882 the watch committee had power to 'at any time suspend and dismiss any borough constable whom they think is negligent in the discharge of his duty or otherwise unfit for the same'. The appellant was dismissed by the committee. No specific charge had been formulated against him. He sought a declaration for the court that his dismissal was illegal and *ultra vires*.	The claimant had the right to a hearing before an unbiased tribunal, the right to know the accusations made against him and the opportunity to answer those allegations.

 **Key debates**

Topic	Doctrine and Theory in Administrative Law: An Elusive Quest for the Limits of Jurisdiction'
Author/Academic	TRS Allan
Viewpoint	Highlights the limitations on the role doctrinal analysis can play in justifying judicial review, with reference to the debate criticizing *ultra vires* and parliamentary intention as the basis for judicial review and seeking to substitute common law doctrine as the foundation of the jurisdiction.
Source	[2003] PL 429–454.

Exam questions

Topic	'Wednesbury's reason and structure
Author/Academic	Paul Daly
Viewpoint	Argues in favour of a redefinition of unreasonableness, focusing on the controversial concept of *Wednesbury* unreasonableness.
Source	(2011, April) PL 238–259

Topic	'Proportionality and the *Human Rights Act 1998*'
Author/Academic	David Feldman
Viewpoint	Discusses the impact and development of the principle of proportionality.
Source	Essay in Evelyn Ellis (ed), *The Principle of Proportionality in the Laws of Europe* (1999) 117, 127 *et seq*.

Topic	'Facing Up to Actual Bias'
Author/Academic	James Goudkamp
Viewpoint	Discusses the reluctance of the courts to consider allegations of actual bias against judges. Outlines the different types of bias which may be alleged and explains that allegations of actual, rather than apparent or presumed bias, are relatively rare.
Source	(2008) 27(1) CJQ 32–39.

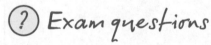 (?) Exam questions

Problem question

Assume that the Financial Institutions Act 2011 (the Act) sets up the Banking Commission (the Commission) and empowers it to nationalize any bank where it is satisfied that any bank is in financial difficulties and there is a danger that its customers will lose their money. The Act provides further that any decision of the Commission must be confirmed by the Secretary of State for Business, Innovation and Skills.

Justin is the managing director of Castlebar Bank plc (the Bank). He learns that the Commission intends to nationalize the Bank. Justin immediately sends a report compiled by the accountants responsible for auditing the Bank's accounts showing that the Bank has an excellent financial record. Justin has, in the past, been highly critical of government economic policy and had opposed the setting up of the Commission. He fears that this might be the real reason for the Commission's decision.

The Commission's decision to nationalize the Bank is confirmed by the Secretary of State for Business, Innovation and Skills following a meeting with the Chancellor of the Exchequer where he is reminded that tighter control of the availability of consumer credit is a fundamental principle of current economic policy.

Advise Justin as to the grounds upon which he might challenge the decision of the Commission and the Secretary of State successfully.

Outline answers are included at the end of the book.

Essay question

Referring to decided cases, critically assess how, if at all, the impact of the principle of proportionality on *Wednesbury* unreasonableness.

 Scan here

Scan this QR code image with your mobile device to see an outline answer to this question or log onto www.oxfordtextbooks.co.uk/orc/concentrate

13

Crown proceedings and public interest immunity

Key Facts

- The **Crown Proceedings Act 1947** forms the procedural basis for civil proceedings against the Crown.

- The Crown, in this context, means the executive or the government.

- The Crown can make contracts with individual persons subject to the same rules and principles governing interpersonal agreements.

- The Crown can avoid contractual liability if payment out of public funds is subsequently not approved by Parliament or if action, which would normally constitute breach of contract, is necessary to protect the welfare of the state.

- If a government department, in its dealings with a private individual, takes it upon itself to assume authority upon a matter with which he is concerned, he is entitled to rely upon it having the authority which it assumes.

- **Section 2 Crown Proceedings Act 1947** extends Crown liability in tort.

- Most, but not all, employment rights contained in the **Employment Rights Act 1996**, as amended, apply to the Crown.

- In cases where the court has to decide whether to allow government documents to be produced in evidence in civil proceedings the court has the power and the duty to balance the public interest asserted by the litigant and the public interest asserted by the government.

Revision tip
When revising this topic it is important to bear in mind that the law can be enforced against the executive in all forms of proceedings. You should link this topic up with the rule of law discussed in chapter 3, human rights discussed in chapter 14 and police powers discussed in chapter 15.

Liability of the Crown in contract

The liability of the Crown in contract is normally governed by the same principles which apply to agreements made by private individuals. This is subject to two common law rules. The first is that an officer appointed by the Crown, negotiating as an agent for the public, is not liable to be sued upon contracts made by him in that capacity.

MacBeath v Haldimand (1786) 99 ER 1036

The claimant was a trader. The defendant was the Governor of Quebec. The defendant, acting as an officer of the crown as the agent for the public, entered into an agreement with the claimant for the supply of goods. A dispute arose concerning the goods supplied and the amount to be paid. The principle from this case was that an officer appointed by the Crown negotiating as an agent for the public, is not liable to be sued upon contracts made by him in that capacity.

The Court of King's Bench held that the defendant was not liable because such wide-ranging personal liability would make public office untenable.

The doctrine was applied in *Dunn v MacDonald* (1897).

Dunn v MacDonald [1897] 1 QB 401

The defendant was the Consul General of an African Colony. He appointed the claimant as an agent for three years. The claimant was dismissed before the expiry date. He claimed breach of an implied warranty that he would be appointed for three years.

The principle from this case was that an agent who makes a contract on behalf of his principal is liable for breach of any implied warranty, concerning his authority to enter into the contract, is not applicable to a contract made by a public servant acting on behalf of the Crown. The court found for the defendant.

Before the **Crown Proceedings Act 1947** there were complex special procedures governing claims for breach of contract against the Crown. The 1947 Act modernized and simplified the procedure. The general principles of Crown Liability in contract were left intact.

The Crown is free to make commercial contracts through its servants. Government departments may be sued for breach of contract. There are two defences. The first is the principle in *Churchward v R* (1865).

Liability of the Crown in contract

****

Churchward v R (1865) LR 1 QB 173

There was a contract for the carriage of mail. The contract expressly provided that payments were to be made out of public funds subject to parliamentary approval. Parliament did not approve.

The principle from this case was that the Crown can escape liability for breach of contract on the basis that Parliament has subsequently voted against providing the money out of public funds. The Crown was held not liable.

> ### Revision Tip
>
> You should compare the defence of executive necessity with the doctrine of estoppel in the form it applies to administrative law.

The second is the defence of executive necessity.

Redriaktiebolaget Amphitrite v The King [1921] 3 KB 500

The claimants were Swedish shipowners who, during the First World War, claimed that the Crown was in breach of contract. The claim was based on two undertakings by British Government officials that their ship would not be detained. The ship was subsequently detained and the shipowners were disqualified from applying for the vessel's release. The principle from this case was that the Crown cannot, by contract, restrain itself from taking necessary executive action concerning the welfare of the state. Rowlatt J gave judgment for the Crown. The principle forming the basis of this decision was affirmed and applied by the Court of Appeal in **Board of Trade v Temperley Steam Shipping Co (1927)**and again, by the Court of Appeal in **Commissioners of Crown Lands v Page (1960)**.

Assumption of responsibility

Public officials may think that they have the power to make a decision which in reality they do not possess. They then go on to act as if they had the power to do so. What happens if a person suffers losses as a result? This was considered in the following case:

Robertson v Minister of Pensions [1949] 1 KB 227

The War Office had jurisdiction over claims in respect of disability attributable to war service. In 1940 jurisdiction over claims in respect of service after 3 September 1939 was transferred to the Minister of Pensions. In 1941 R, who was a serving officer, wrote to the War Office regarding a disability which had resulted from an injury in December 1939. He received a reply stating that his disability had been accepted as attributable to military service. Relying on that assurance, he decided not to obtain an independent medical opinion. The Minister later decided that the disability was not attributable to war service but to an injury sustained in 1927. R appealed to the High Court from a decision of a pensions tribunal, which agreed with the Minister's decision. The principle from this case was if a government department, in its dealings with citizens, takes it upon itself to assume authority upon a matter with which he is concerned, he is entitled to rely upon it having the authority which it assumes. The government department is bound. Denning J set aside the decision of the tribunal.

Liability of the Crown in tort

Revision tip

Crown liability in tort is limited in many ways. These limitations have important human rights implications for governmental liability. This topic provides a foundation for the study of governmental liability in the **Human Rights Act 1998** in chapter 14.

The Crown is subject to liability in tort under **s 2 Crown Proceedings Act 1947**. The Crown is liable for torts committed by its servants or agents; breach of duties owed to employees; and breach of any duty arising out of ownership, occupation, possession, or control of property. The Crown has the benefit of any defence to which its employees, servants and agents are entitled. In addition under **s 2(4)** of the **1947 Act**, the Crown has the benefit of any statutory restriction on the liability of any government department or officer.

In *Home Office v Dorset Yacht Club* (1970) the House of Lords had to decide whether the claimants, who had suffered physical damage to their property caused by borstal boys in the custody of Crown servants, could sue the Home Office in the tort of negligence. The Home Office was held to owe a duty of care to the claimants.

Special provisions, under the **Crown Proceedings (Armed Forces) Act 1987** apply where any member of the armed forces suffers death or personal injury, in pensionable service while on duty, caused by another member of the armed forces. There will be no Crown liability in tort if there is any imminent national danger or great emergency; or if the damage is sustained in any warlike activity outside the United Kingdom.

The Crown as an employer

Revision tip

You should determine whether and to what extent a Crown employee has the same rights as other employees.

At common law the 'employment' rights of Crown servants were limited. They certainly did not enjoy the same degree of security of tenure as other categories of workers.

Dunn v The Queen [1896] 1 QB 116

The Consul General of the Niger Protectorate in Africa, acting on behalf of the Crown, appointed Dunn to be a consular agent in Crown service for three years. He was dismissed before the period had expired. Dunn claimed damages from the Crown.

✳✳✳✳✳✳✳✳✳✳✳

The principle from this case was that in all but the most exceptional cases it is essential for the public good that Crown employment should be capable of being determined at will. The claimant's action failed.

Employment legislation and the Crown

The **Employment Rights Act 1996**, as amended, is the primary source of law. Most, but not all, employment rights secured by this Act apply to the Crown. They apply to civil servants but not to the armed forces. Moreover, the redundancy payments scheme, in the Act, does not bind the Crown. Civil Servants may claim unfair dismissal. Crown employees are protected by the **Equal Pay Act 1970**, the **Sex Discrimination Act 1975**, and the **Public Interest Disclosure Act 1998**.

Public interest immunity

Revision tip

One of the problems with commencing civil proceedings against government departments is that vital evidence might be contained in documents to which the claimant has no automatic right of access. You should revise this area in connection with freedom of information and human rights.

In legal actions taken against ministers and government departments, evidence for the claimant's case may include government documents and Cabinet papers.

In the House of Lords' decision in *Conway v Rimmer* (1968) it was determined that a court has no power to compel disclosure of such documents. But they may be disclosed, if it is found that disclosure will not be prejudicial to the **public interest**. In general, disclosure should be ordered when harm will not be done to the nation or the public service by the disclosure of the documents; and the administration of justice will be frustrated if they are withheld.

Their production will not be ordered if the possible injury to the nation or the public service is so grave that no other interest should be allowed to prevail over it, but, where the possible injury is substantially less, the court must balance against each other the two public interests involved. When a minister's certificate suggests that the document belongs to a class which ought to be withheld, then, unless his reasons are of a kind that judicial experience is not competent to weigh, the proper test is whether the withholding of a document of that particular class is really necessary for the functioning of the public service. If on balance, considering the likely importance of the document in the case before it, the court considers that it should probably be produced, it should generally examine the document before ordering the production.

The party seeking production had to show that the documents were likely to assist his case.

Air Canada v Secretary of State (No 2) [1983] 2 AC 394

In 1979 and 1980 the BAA substantially increased landing charges at Heathrow. The claimants were a group of airlines. They claimed that the increases were excessive and discriminatory. They brought an action claiming that the Secretary of State's order for the increases was *ultra vires*. The claimants sought discovery of documents relating to communications between ministers concerning the formulation of government policy. The Secretary of State claimed immunity from disclosure in the public interest. The Court of Appeal and the House of Lords refused to allow discovery.

Official secrets

Section 1 Official Secrets Act 1989 provides that a person who has either been a member of the security and intelligence services or notified that they are subject to requirements of the Act will be guilty of a criminal offence if they disclose information concerning their work.

Freedom of information

Section 1 Freedom of Information Act 2000 provides that any person making a request for information to a public authority is entitled to be informed in writing by the public authority whether it holds information of the description specified in the request, and if that is the case to have that information communicated to him.

Part II of the Act contains wide-ranging exemptions which limit the scope of this right. **Section 2** provides that where any provision of **Pt II** states that the duty to confirm or deny does not arise in relation to any information, the effect of the provision is that where either- the provision confers absolute exemption, orin all the circumstances of the case, the public interest in maintaining the exclusion of the duty to confirm or deny outweighs the public interest in disclosing whether the public authority holds the information, **s 1(1)(a)** does not apply.

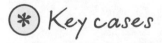 **(✱) Key cases**

Case	Facts	Principle
Churchward v R (1865) LR 1 QB 173	There was a contract for the carriage of mail. The contract expressly provided that payments were to be made out of public funds subject to parliamentary approval.	The Crown can escape liability for breach of contract on the basis that Parliament has subsequently voted against providing the money out of public funds.

Key cases

****

Case	Facts	Principle
Conway v Rimmer [1968] AC 910	The House of Lords had to decide whether government documents could be produced in civil proceedings when the government claimed Crown privilege.	In civil litigation, where the question is whether government documents should be produced in evidence, the court has the power and the duty to weigh the public interest of justice to litigants against the public interest asserted by the government. In many cases this can be done only by inspecting the documents, which can properly be shown to the court but not to the parties, before the court decides whether to order production.
Home Office v Dorset Yacht Club [1970] AC 1004	The House of Lords had to decide whether the claimants, who had suffered physical damage to their property, caused by borstal boys in the custody of Crown servants, could sue the Home Office in the tort of negligence.	The Crown servants owed a duty of care based on *Donoghue v Stevenson* (1932) principles.
MacBeath v Haldimand (1786) 99 ER 1036	The claimant was a trader. The defendant was the Governor of Quebec. The defendant, acting as an officer of the crown acting as an agent for the public, entered into an agreement with the claimant for the supply of goods. A dispute arose concerning the goods supplied and the amount to be paid.	An officer appointed by the Crown negotiating as an agent for the public, is not liable to be sued upon contracts made by him in that capacity.
Redriaktiebolaget Amphitrite v The King [1921] 3 KB 500	The claimants were Swedish shipowners, during the First World War, who claimed that the Crown was in breach of contract. The claim was based on two undertakings by British Government officials that their ship would not be detained. The ship was subsequently detained and the shipowners were disqualified from applying for the vessel's release.	The Crown cannot, by contract, restrain itself from taking necessary executive action concerning the welfare of the state.

 **Key debates**

Topic	'Opening the Cabinet Door: Freedom of Information and government policy making'
Author/Academic	Robert Hazell
Viewpoint	Provides a comparison between the freedom of information regimes in the UK, Australia, Canada, Ireland, and New Zealand.
Source	(2011, April) PL 260–283.

Topic	'Compensation and the Armed Forces: The New No Fault Scheme'
Author/Academic	Hilary Meredit
Viewpoint	Examines claims made under the Armed Forces Compensation Scheme, introduced on 6 April 2005. Explains the scheme in terms of tariff, guaranteed income payments for life, abatement, and compensation. Includes a table outlining the level of payments for particular categories under the scheme and provides examples of claims settled under common law.
Source	(2006) 2 Journal of Personal Injury Law 171–179.

Topic	'1987 Crown Immunity: Putting the Tin Hat on Ex-servicemen's Immunity was Upheld'
Author/Academic	Richard Scorer
Viewpoint	Comments on the European Court of Human Rights ruling in **Roche v United Kingdom (32555/96)** on whether the pre-1987 Crown immunity, in relation to acts or omissions involving members of the armed forces occurring before the date that **s 10 Crown Proceedings Act 1947** was repealed by the **Crown Proceedings (Armed Forces) Act 1987**, breached the **European Convention on Human Rights 1950**.
Source	(2006) 42(Feb) PILJ 15–17.

Topic	'Crown: Remedies in Proceedings against Crown – Crown Proceedings Act'
Author/Academic	Case comment
Viewpoint	Notes the House of Lords' ruling in **Davidson v Scottish Ministers (No 1) (2006)** on whether the court had jurisdiction under **s 21 Crown Proceedings Act 1947** to grant an interim or final interdict, or an interim or final order for specific performance in proceedings against the Crown.
Source	[2006] PL 386–387.

Exam questions

✶✶✶✶✶✶✶✶✶✶✶✶

Topic	'Combat Immunity and the Duty of Care'
Author/Academic	James Rowley
Viewpoint	Examines the Queen's Bench ruling in *Multiple Claimants v Ministry of Defence* (2003) on the basis of combat immunity, the geographical and operational scope of the immunity, the temporal and operational scope of the immunity, qualification for actual operations against the enemy, whether sailing or driving without due care and attention attracted immunity, the application of immunity to anti-terrorist, policing and peacekeeping operations, the effect of the breach occurring outside the operation of the immunity, and whether immunity attached by reason of the injury occurring at a time when the immunity conditions attached.
Source	(2004) 4 JPI Law 280–290.

 Exam questions

Essay question 1

Explain the principles upon which Crown servants may own a duty of care in the tort of negligence.

Essay question 2

Critically explain the rules governing disclosure of documents in Crown Proceedings and the rights of citizens to obtain information from public authorities under the **Freedom of Information Act 2000**.

 Scan here

Scan this QR code image with your mobile device to see outline answers to these questions or log onto www.oxfordtextbooks.co.uk/orc/concentrate

#14
Introduction to human rights in UK law

Key Facts

- Before the **Human Rights Act (HRA) 1998**, civil and political rights were recognized and enforced in the United Kingdom solely within the established framework of statutory and common law principles.

- During the twentieth century, human rights principles were developed in international law by the law of treaties and by international organizations.

- The Council of Europe drafted the **European Convention on Human Rights and Fundamental Freedoms** to guarantee basic civil and political rights, which have been expanded by a series of supplementary treaties called protocols, and provide a judicial system for their enforcement.

- The European Convention is a treaty and, as such, could not give individual citizens directly enforceable rights until the 'Convention rights' were incorporated by the **HRA 1998**.

- A poor record in the European Court of Human Rights, human rights problems in the English courts, and worries about the relationship between the executive and Parliament provide the background to the Act.

- The **HRA 1998** incorporates 'Convention rights' into UK law.

- The **HRA 1998** creates new rules of statutory interpretation, enables citizens to test the compatibility of legislation with Convention rights, and obliges the courts to take 'Strasbourg principles' into account when considering human rights issues in litigation.

- The **HRA 1998** makes it unlawful for a public authority to act in any way which is incompatible with Convention rights, allows individuals to rely on breach of convention rights in any proceedings brought against public authorities and provides some extra remedies.

Human rights and English law

Revision tip

You should begin looking at this subject by reviewing how human rights principles are embedded into English common law and statute.

Before the **HRA 1998** came into force, human rights protection in the United Kingdom was based on remedies contained in specific causes of action or penalties available through the criminal justice system.

International law has had a considerable influence on the development of human rights law. The twentieth century saw the formation of international organizations, committed to the promotion of human rights, and the growth of a conceptual network of treaties which created human rights rules and principles.

The European Convention on Human Rights and Fundamental Freedoms

Revision tip

You should have a working knowledge of the content of the European Convention and link it to your revision of **s 1 and Sch 1 HRA 1998**.

The **European Convention on Human Rights and Fundamental Freedoms** guarantees civil and political rights. These are the right to life; the prohibition of torture, inhuman, and degrading treatment or punishment; the prohibition of slavery and forced labour; the right to liberty; the right to a fair and unbiased hearing; the prohibition of retrospective legislation; the right to respect for private and family life; freedom of conscience and religion; freedom of expression; freedom of association; the right to marry and found a family.

The **European Convention on Human Rights and Fundamental Freedoms** has been supplemented and amended by a series of additional treaties called protocols. The First and Sixth Protocols give individuals additional rights which were incorporated into British law by the **HRA 1998**.

The First Protocol covers the protection of property; the right to education; and the right to free elections. The Sixth and Twelfth Protocols cover the abolition of the death penalty.

✔ *Looking for extra marks?*

The reasons for the decision to incorporate the European Convention into British law include problems with the UK human rights record both in the British courts and the European Court of Human Rights. You should refer to your recommended standard textbook and read some of the cases contributing to this debate.

Human Rights Act 1998

The first thing the Act does is create '**Convention rights**'. These are defined in **s 1** and set out
in **Sch 1** of the Act. They are **Articles 2 to 12**, **Article 14**, and the **First and Sixth Protocols**.
Under **s 2**, the courts are obliged to take into account all the jurisprudence of the European
Court of Human Rights when considering a claim involving a Convention right.

Proportionality

In the context of judicial review, this principle has had a significant effect on the development of the law. This, and the relevant case law, was discussed in chapter 12. The court considers what is necessary to achieve the legitimate aims of a particular policy or legislation.
This was the case in the House of Lords' decision in the following case.

R (Daly) v Secretary of State for the Home Department [2001] 2 AC 532

The applicant was a prisoner. He kept correspondence with his solicitor in his cell. Every day his
cell was searched. In accordance with rules made under s **47(1) Prison Act 1952**, he was excluded
from his cell while the search was conducted. Officers could examine, but not read, any legally
privileged correspondence to check that nothing had been written on it by the prisoner, or stored
between its pages, likely to endanger prison security. The applicant sought judicial review of the
decision to require examination of prisoners' legally privileged correspondence in their absence.
The principle from this case was that a person sentenced to a custodial order retains the right to
communicate confidentially with a legal adviser under the seal of legal professional privilege. Such
rights can be curtailed only by clear and express words and then only to the extent reasonably necessary to meet the ends which justify the curtailment. It was held that the policy was an unlawful
intrusion into personal privacy protected by **Article 8(1) ECHR** and amounted to a breach of legal
professional privilege. The reasons for the policy went beyond what was necessary to achieve the
legitimate aims of s **47(1)**. It was also beyond what was necessary to satisfy **Article 8(2) ECHR**.

In addition to this, proportionality often involves striking a balance between the benefits
to be achieved by doing something and the harm that may be done by interfering with a
person's Convention rights in the process. This was considered by the House of Lords, in the
context of **Article 8 ECHR** in *Campbell v MGN Ltd* (2004).

Campbell v MGN [2004] 2 AC 457

The claimant was a model who claimed that her privacy had been violated by the publication
of details concerning treatment she had received for drug addiction and rehabilitation. The

House of Lords had to consider the claimant's right to privacy set against the right to freedom of expression.

The House of Lords laid down the following principles. The exercise of balancing **Article 8** and **Article 10** may begin when the person publishing the information knows or ought to know that there is a reasonable expectation that the information in question will be kept confidential. Once the information is identified as 'private' in this way, the court must balance the claimant's interest in keeping the information private against the countervailing interest of the recipient in publishing it. When two Convention rights are in play, the proportionality of interfering with one has to be balanced against the proportionality of restricting the other. The court looks at the comparative importance of the actual rights being claimed in the individual case; the justifications for interfering with or restricting each of those rights; and apply the proportionality test to each.

It was held by the House of Lords that in the circumstances the claimant's right to privacy protected by **Article 8** was violated because the publications amounted to a breach of confidence.

. . . .

Section 3 requires the courts to interpret primary and secondary legislation in a manner which is compatible with Convention rights so far as it is possible to do so. The **s 3** requirement was interpreted and applied by the House of Lords in *R v A* **(2002)**.

. . . .

R v A [2002] 1 AC 45

The House of Lords was asked to interpret **s 41 Youth Justice and Criminal Evidence Act 1999** in a manner which is consistent with **Article 6 ECHR**. The section concerns the admissibility of evidence in rape cases relating to consent. The House of Lords laid down the following principle. Bearing in mind the legitimate aim of protecting the complainant from indignity and humiliating questioning, the test of admissibility in **s 41**, when interpreted, applying the interpretative obligation under **s 3 HRA 1998**, is whether the evidential material was nevertheless so relevant to the issue of consent that to exclude it would endanger the fairness of the trial under **Article 6**. Where that test is satisfied the evidence should not be excluded. The appeal was dismissed.

. . . .

The judicial use of **s 3** is illustrated by the House of Lords' decision in *Ghaidan v Godin-Mendoza* **(2004)** (see chapter 8). It is also illustrated, in relation to **s 23 Anti-terrorism, Crime and Security Act 2001** in *A and Others v Secretary of State for the Home Department* **(2005)** (see chapter 15).

With regard to legislation which post-dates the Act, the minister introducing the bill has to issue a 'statement of compatibility' ie that the bill is compatible with the Convention rights.

Using the Convention against public authorities

Revision tip

When answering problem questions you will have to determine whether the defendant is a public authority within the meaning of **s 6(3)**. This is a tricky issue and you should revise the relevant case law carefully.

It is unlawful for a public authority to act in a way which is incompatible with a Convention right. This provision is contained in **s 6(1)** of the **1998 Act**. A public authority, according to **s 6(3)**, includes a court or tribunal; and any person certain of whose functions are functions of a public nature. It does not, according to **s 6(3)**, include either House of Parliament or a person exercising functions in connection with proceedings in Parliament.

The meaning of '**public authority**' was discussed by the House of Lords in *L v Birmingham City Council* **(2008)** (see key cases).

Under **s 7(1)** any **victim** (or 'would be' victim) of an unlawful act under **s 6(1)** may bring proceedings against the authority in any appropriate court or tribunal, or rely on the Convention right or rights concerned in any legal proceedings.

Proceedings must, under **s 7(5)** be brought within one year beginning with the date on which the act complained of took place; or such longer period as the court or tribunal considers equitable in all the circumstances. Shorter time limits apply as in judicial review.

'Victim' means anyone who is directly affected by the act or the omission that is the subject of the complaint. The extent of a person's right to rely on a breach of a Convention right was discussed by the House of Lords in the following case.

Matthews v Ministry of Defence [2003] 1 AC 1163

The claimant claimed damages in the tort of negligence. The defendant sought to escape liability by relying on **s 10 Crown Proceedings Act 1947**. The case raised a preliminary issue as to whether **s 10 of the Act** was compatible with the right to a fair trial contained in **Article 6 European Convention on Human Rights and Fundamental Freedoms**. The principle from this case was that although the meaning of 'civil rights' in **Article 6 of the Convention**, is an autonomous concept and cannot be interpreted solely by reference to domestic law, a litigant's right of access to the court under **Article 6(1)** applies only to civil rights which could, on arguable grounds, be recognized under domestic law and where the restriction on the right of access was procedural in nature. It was held that **s 10** imposed a limitation which operated not as a procedural bar but as a matter of substantive law under which the claimant had no civil right to which **Article 6** might apply.

Remedies

If a public authority has breached a Convention right, the remedy, which the court can grant to the victim is covered by **s 8**. The remedies available under **s 8(1)** are familiar: damages, declarations, injunctions, quashing orders, mandatory orders, and prohibiting orders.

Damages

The availability of damages under **s 8** was discussed by the House of Lords in the following case:

Marcic v Thames Water Utility [2004] 2 AC 42

The defendant is a statutory sewerage undertaker under the **Water Industry Act 1991** and, as such, is a public authority under **s 6(3) HRA 1998**. The claimant was a householder whose premises were regularly flooded with sewage. He claimed damages in nuisance and under the **HRA 1998**. The principle from this case was that where a public authority is subject to an elaborate statutory scheme of regulation, which includes an independent regulator with powers of enforcement whose decisions are subject to judicial review, there is no claim for damages under **s 6(1) HRA 1998**.

It was held that the claimant had no claim for damages against Thames Water.

. . . .

The approach to awarding damages in human rights cases was determined in the following case:

. . . .

Anufrijeva v Southwark [2004] 2 WLR 603

This appeal arose out of three cases each of which was a claim for damages for breach of privacy under **Article 8 ECHR**. The Court of Appeal had to consider the rules determining awards of damages in England and Wales where **s 8** Convention rights are engaged.

The principle from this case was that the approach to awarding damages in this jurisdiction should be no less liberal than those applied by the European Court of Human Rights or one of the purposes of the **1998 Act** will be defeated and claimants will still be put to the expense of having to go to Strasbourg to obtain just satisfaction.

Under **s 8 HRA 1998**, damages can be awarded on the basis of what is necessary and appropriate to give just satisfaction. Such awards should be modest. Where there is a claim for damages under **s 8 HRA 1998** involving maladministration, appropriate procedures should be followed to ensure that the cost of obtaining relief is proportionate to the amount of compensation being claimed.

It was held that on the facts in each case, there had been no breach of the claimants' right to privacy.

. . . .

The House of Lords considered the level of awards of damages and the effect of the jurisprudence of the European Court of Human Rights in *R v Secretary of State for the Home Department, ex p Greenfield* (2005). The House of Lords stated the following principles concerning awards of damages under s 8 HRA 1998. In deciding, under s 8 HRA 1998, whether an award of damages is necessary to give just satisfaction for violations of Article 6, and if so how much, the British courts had to look to the jurisprudence of the European Court of Human Rights for guidance.The focus of the **European Convention on Human Rights and Fundamental Freedoms** is the protection of human rights rather than awards of compensation. This is reflected in the approach of the European Court of Human Rights, which is to treat the finding that Article 6 has been violated as in itself giving just satisfaction to the injured party, and not to speculate on what the outcome of the particular proceedings would have been if the violation had not occurred. The European Court will award damages only where it is satisfied that the loss or damage complained of is actually caused by the violation, although it has on occasions been willing in appropriate cases to make an award where it is deprived of a real chance of a better outcome. Awards of compensation for anxiety and frustration attributable to the **Article 6** violation suffered are made very sparingly and for modest sums. Awards are not precisely calculated but are such as were judged by the court to be fair and equitable in particular cases. Although judges in England and Wales are not inflexibly bound by awards of the European Court of Human Rights, they should not aim to be significantly more or less generous than that court might be expected to be if it were willing to make an award at all.

Injunctions

It is necessary to consider the effect of **s 12(3) and (4) HRA 1998** where an injunction is sought to restrain publication of any material and the issue is whether this would violate **Article 10 ECHR** which guarantees freedom of speech. The court may also have to consider **Article 8** where the claimant says that publication of material amounts to breach of privacy. This was discussed in **Douglas v Hello Ltd (2001)**. The Court of Appeal applied the following principles. Where a court has to decide whether to grant an injunction, which might affect the exercise of the right to freedom of expression protected by **Article 10 ECHR**, it must, in accordance with **s 12(4) HRA 1998**, look at the importance of that right. Moreover, the qualifications set out in **Article 10(2)** are as relevant as, and entitled to no less regard than, the right set out in **Article 10(1)**. When determining, in accordance with **s 12(3)** whether it is likely to be established at trial that publication should not be allowed, the court should take into account the full range of relevant Convention rights, including the right to respect for private and family life protected by **Article 8**. **Section 12(3)** requires the court, before it grants an injunction to restrain publication, to consider the merits of the case and seek to balance the merits of one right against another without giving undue weight to either of them. The principles of legality and proportionality must be used to articulate the rights involved and to determine whether it is possible to strike a balance in favour of restraint of publication.

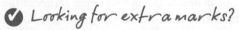 ✅ *Looking for extra marks?*

The judges in *Douglas v Hello Ltd* (2001) made some significant comments concerning Article 8 and its effect on English law. You should look this case up and read their judgments.

Declarations of Incompatibility

Revision tip

You will find that **s 4 HRA 1998** has implications for parliamentary sovereignty and judicial review. You should revise this topic in conjunction with chapter 8 and chapter 12. This will help you to understand it in greater depth.

Section 4 of the Act creates the 'declaration of incompatibility'. The most important effect of making a declaration is that it puts pressure on the government to change the law. The courts which have power to make such declarations are the House of Lords, the Judicial Committee of the Privy Council, the Courts-Martial Appeal Court, the High Court of Justiciary, the

Court of Session, the High Court, and the Court of Appeal. It is important to note that declarations of incompatibility are not available in county courts, tribunals, the Crown Court, or magistrates' courts. Principles governing declarations of incompatibility were discussed by the Court of Appeal in the following case.

Wilson v First Country Trust Limited (No 2) [2001] 3 WLR 42

The Court of Appeal ordered a hearing in order to determine whether to make a declaration of incompatibility under s **4(2) HRA 1998** that **s 127 Consumer Credit Act 1974** was incompatible with **Article 6 ECHR** and **Article 1 of the First Protocol** in that it barred a creditor from enforcing a loan agreement.

Ever since 1 October 2000, the court is required by the provisions of the **HRA 1998** to avoid acting in a way which is incompatible with a Convention right. The court must consider: (1) the facts as they were at the time when it made the order; and, whether that obligation is affected by **s 22(4) HRA 1998**, which prevents a claimant from relying on the **1998 Act** where a public authority has acted incompatibly with a Convention rights prior to 1 October 1998; and (2) the relevant date for deciding whether **s 22(4)** applies is the date the court made the order. The court had power to make a declaration of incompatibility pursuant to **s 4 HRA 1998**.

The principles governing declarations of incompatibility were developed further in *R (Alconbury Developments Limited) v Secretary of State for the Environment, Transport and the Regions* **(2001).** The House of Lords laid down the following principles. To determine whether civil rights under **Article 6(1) ECHR** are involved in a claim, the court must look at the relevant jurisprudence of the European Court of Human Rights. A Secretary of State is not an independent and impartial tribunal.Decisions taken by a Secretary of State are compatible with **Article 6(1)** provided they are reviewable by an independent and impartial tribunal which has full jurisdiction to deal with the case as the nature of the decision requires. If the decision is one of administrative policy the reviewing body is not required to have full power to re-determine the merits of the decision and any review by a court of the merits of such a policy decision, taken by a minister answerable to Parliament and ultimately to the electorate, would be profoundly undemocratic. The power of the High Court in judicial review proceedings to review the legality of the decision and the procedures followed is sufficient to ensure compatibility with **Article 6(1). Section 10** provides for a so-called 'fast track' procedure for the amendment of legislation, which has been declared to be incompatible with a Convention right. The Minister can amend legislation.

What are the consequences of a declaration of incompatibility?

Such a declaration may be thought to carry some moral pressure and could not be ignored; but perhaps a government could ignore it on reflection. But such a declaration is most likely to be followed by amending legislation invoking the remedial orders under **s 10**.

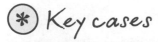 **Key cases**

Case	Facts	Principle
Douglas v Hello! Ltd [2001] 2 WLR 992	This was an application for an injunction to restrain publication of unauthorized wedding photographs.	The Court of Appeal laid down principles relating to s 12 HRA 1998.
L v Birmingham City Council [2008] 1 AC 95	The question was whether the owners and proprietors of a care home who took people on behalf of a local authority was a public authority for the purposes of s 6 HRA 1998.	The provision of care and accommodation by a private company, as opposed to its regulation and supervision under statutory rules, is not an inherently public function and fell outside the ambit of s 6(3)(b).
R v A [2002] 1 AC 45	The House of Lords was asked to interpret s 41 Youth Justice and Criminal Evidence Act 1999 in a manner which is consistent with Article 6 European Convention on Human Rights and Fundamental Freedoms. The section concerns the admissibility of evidence in rape cases relating to consent.	Bearing in mind the legitimate aim of protecting the complainant from indignity and humiliating questioning, the test of admissibility in s 41, when interpreted applying the interpretative obligation under s 3 HRA 1998, is whether the evidential material was nevertheless so relevant to the issue of consent that to exclude it would endanger the fairness of the trial under Article 6. Where that test is satisfied the evidence should not be excluded.
R v Secretary of State for the Home Department, ex p Greenfield [2005] 1 WLR 673	The claimant was a prisoner who applied for judicial review of the deputy controller's decisions, contending that they infringed his right to a fair trial under Article 6 of the European Convention for the Protection of Human Rights and Fundamental Freedoms, as scheduled to the HRA 1998. He sought damages for violations of Article 6.	The House of Lords laid down significant principles concerning awards of damages under s 8 HRA 1998.

Key debates

✱✱✱✱✱✱✱✱✱✱✱✱

Case	Facts	Principle
R (Alconbury Developments Limited) v Secretary of State for the Environment, Transport and the Regions [2001] 2 WLR 1389	This case concerned several powers granted to the Secretary of State by the Transport and Works Act 1992, the Town and Country Planning Act 1990, the Highways Act 1980, and the Acquisition of Land Act 1981. The claimants sought declarations of incompatibility under s 4 HRA 1998 on the ground that they were incompatible with Article 6 of the European Convention.	The impugned powers of the Secretary of State were not incompatible with Article 6(1).

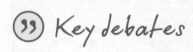 **Key debates**

Topic	'Taking the next step? Achieving another Bill of Rights'
Author/ Academic	Colin Harvey
Viewpoint	Examines the debate over the potential implementation of a new UK constitutional Bill of Rights in terms of what it may mean in practice.
Source	(2011) 1 European Human Rights Law Review, 24–42.

Topic	'The Right to a Fair Trial and the Arbitration Act 1996: Apparent Conflicts Leave the English Courts Unmoved'
Author/ Academic	Paul Stothard
Viewpoint	Assesses the approach of the courts to the application of **Article 6 European Convention on Human Rights 1950** to commercial arbitration proceedings in England and Wales, falling under courts' supervision by virtue of the **Arbitration Act 1996**. Considers the **HRA 1998** and the right of access to a court under **Article 6**, commercial arbitration, and civil rights, the waiver of **Article 6**, case law guidance on the impact of **Article 6** on arbitration, and **Article 6** and the court's supervisory procedure. Argues that it is unlikely that **Article 6** can be regarded as a basis to challenge an arbitration agreement.
Source	(2008) 29(1) Bus LR 2–6.

Key debates

✳✳✳✳✳✳✳✳✳✳✳✳✳

Topic	'The Executive, the Parole Board and Article 5 ECHR: Progress within "An Unhappy State of Affairs"?'
Author/ Academic	Patricia Londono
Viewpoint	Discusses the Court of Appeal decisions in: (1) *R (on the application of Brooke) v Parole Board* (2008)on whether the Parole Board was sufficiently independent to meet the requirements of **Article 5(4)** and (2) **European Convention on Human Rights 1950**; and (2) *R (on the application of Walker) v Secretary of State for the Home Department* (2008) on whether failure to provide offenders imprisoned for public protection with rehabilitation programmes to assist them to demonstrate that their detention was no longer necessary was unlawful and their continued detention after expiry of their minimum term infringed **Article 5**.
Source	(2008) 67(2) Cambridge Law Journal 230–233.

Topic	'Negligence Liability for Failing to Prevent Crime: The Human Rights Dimension'
Author/ Academic	Iain Steele
Viewpoint	Comments on the Court of Appeal decision in *Smith v Chief Constable of Sussex* (2008) on whether a man who allegedly told police of threats made against him by a former partner, could sue them in negligence after he was attacked by that person on the grounds that they did nothing to protect him. Reviews the court's approach to the principles set out by the House of Lords in *Hill v Chief Constable of West Yorkshire* (1989) and its analysis of the subsequent impact of the HRA 1998 on common law negligence actions against the police. Notes the forthcoming appeal to the House of Lords.
Source	(2008) 67(2) Cambridge Law Journal 239–241.

Topic	'May Day, May Day: Policing Protest.'
Author/ Academic	ATH Smith
Viewpoint	Discusses the Court of Appeal decision in *Austin v Commissioner of Police of the Metropolis* (2007) on whether the police had been justified in depriving the claimants of their liberty, by cordoning them within an area for seven hours along with over 1,000 protestors, on the ground that it was necessary to prevent a breach of the peace. Considers whether the defendant was required to prove that the claimants had behaved unlawfully or had threatened to breach the peace. Assesses whether the deprivation of liberty was such that it breached the claimants' rights under **Article 5 European Convention on Human Rights 1950**.
Source	(2008) 67(1) Cambridge Law Journal 10–12.

Exam questions

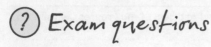

Essay question 1

Explain what is meant by 'Convention right' and how the **Human Rights Act 1998** incorporates such rights into British law.

Essay question 2

Critically assess the roles of Parliament, the executive, and the judiciary in the enforcement of human rights.

 Scan here
Scan this QR code image with your mobile device to see outline answers to these questions or log onto www.oxfordtextbooks.co.uk/orc/concentrate

#15

Police powers, public order, and terrorism

Key Facts

- Police officers detect and prevent crime, bring offenders to justice, keep the peace, and protect people and their property from injury and damage.

- The **Police and Criminal Evidence Act 1984**, as amended, and its Codes of Practice, contain rules concerning police powers of stop, search, entry, seizure of property, arrest, detention, and treatment of suspects.

- The **Public Order Act 1986** concerns the control of protests and assemblies.

- Police powers contained in the **1986 Act** were extended by the **Criminal Justice and Public Order Act 1994** and the **Anti-social Behaviour Act 2003**.

- The **Serious Organised Crime and Police Act 2005** made important changes to the rules governing powers of arrest and introduced further restrictions to the right to protest in parts of Central London.

- The **Terrorism Act 2000** introduced comprehensive counter-terrorist measures throughout the United Kingdom.

- The **Anti-terrorism Crime and Security Act 2001** focuses on terrorist funding, intelligence gathering, immigration, and the elimination of organized crime.

- The **Terrorism Act 2006** extends the law further.

Police powers

In the House of Lords' decision in *Brooks v Commissioner of Police of the Metropolis* (2005) Lord Steyn said that the prime function of the police is the preservation of the Queen's peace. The police prevent crime, protect life and property, apprehend criminals, and preserve evidence.

The Police and Criminal Evidence Act 1984 (PACE), as amended, and the codes of practice made under it contain rules concerning stop and search (**ss 1–7**); entry, search, and seizure of property (**ss 8–23**); arrest (**ss 24–33**); detention (**ss 34–51**); and treatment of suspects (**ss 53–65**).

The Codes of Practice

Code A deals with stop and search powers prior to making an arrest. **Code B** deals with the power to enter and search premises and seize property. **Code C** concerns detention, treatment, and questioning of non-terrorist suspects. **Code D** deals with identification of wanted persons and the keeping of accurate and reliable criminal records. **Code E** deals with the tape recording of interviews with suspects in the police station. **Code F** deals with the visual recording with sound of interviews with suspects. **Code G** deals with powers of arrest. **Code H** sets out the requirements for the detention, treatment, and questioning of suspects related to terrorism in police custody.

Stop and search

Acting on reasonable suspicion a police officer may stop and search anyone in order find stolen goods, drugs, an offensive weapon, any article made or adapted for use in certain offences, for example a burglary or theft, knives, or any items which could damage or destroy property. This includes spray paint cans. A police officer may use reasonable force if the person being searched will not cooperate. Force, however, should be used only as a last resort.

In *R v Bristol (Christopher)* (2007) the Court of Appeal had to decide whether a drug search was unlawful because the police officer failed, before commencing the search, to take the reasonable steps required by **s 2 PACE**. This section requires a police constable to give his name and the name of the police station to which he is attached. The Court of Appeal held that the search was unlawful and the conviction was quashed.

The power to enter and search premises

Police officers may enter and search premises if they have obtained a search warrant, or have a statutory right to enter and search, or have obtained the permission of the owner or occupier.

If they have a search warrant, the police must search the premises at a reasonable hour and, if the owner is in occupation, with their cooperation. When they seek entry to any private premises, the police officers must identify themselves (and, if they are not in uniform, show their warrant card) and explain why they want to search, the rights of the occupier, and whether the search is made with a search warrant or not. Having obtained a search warrant the police may force entry if the occupier has refused entry, or it is impossible to communicate with the occupier, or the occupier is absent, or the premises are unoccupied, or they have reasonable grounds for believing that if they do not force entry it would hinder the search, or someone would be placed in danger.

Police officers have statutory authority to enter private premises without a warrant in order to deal with a breach of the peace or prevent it, enforce an arrest warrant, arrest a person in connection with certain offences, recapture someone who has escaped from custody, or save life or prevent serious damage to property. Unless entering premises to save life or protect property, a police officer must have reasonable grounds to believe that the person for whom they are searching is there. Police officers may search premises occupied by an arrested person or visited by an arrested person during or immediately prior to their arrest. The police must reasonably believe that they might find evidence connected with the crime an arrested person is accused of committing.

Seizure of property

Police officers should seize goods only if they have reasonable grounds to believe that the goods have been obtained illegally; or are evidence in relation to an offence. The police must also have reasonable grounds to believe that it is necessary to seize the goods to prevent them being lost, stolen, or destroyed.

Arrest

If a private citizen arrests anyone, they must inform the arrested person of the charge or the crime he is suspected of having committed. A police officer arresting someone without warrant must tell the arrested person the charge upon which the arrest is being made or the facts which are said to constitute the crime he is alleged to have committed.

This information must be given to the person being arrested at the time of his arrest or at the first reasonable opportunity after the arrest. This was determined by the House of Lords in *Christie v Leachinsky* (1947).

Police officers can arrest a person if they have a warrant. They may arrest a person without warrant if they have reasonable grounds to suspect that the person being arrested has committed certain offences; is committing certain offences; is about to commit certain offences.

✳✳✳✳✳✳✳✳✳✳✳✳

The **Serious Organised Crime and Police Act 2005** gives police officers the power to arrest a person to find out the person's name and address. A person may also be arrested to prevent them causing physical injury to themselves or any other person; suffering physical injury; causing loss of or damage to property; committing an offence against public decency; or causing an unlawful obstruction of the highway. Police officers may also make an arrest in order to protect a child or other vulnerable person; allow the prompt and effective investigation of the offence the arrested person is suspected of committing or the conduct which has prompted their arrest; and prevent any prosecution for the offence from being hindered by the disappearance of the person being arrested.

Detention

At the police station, the arrested person has the right to: inform someone of their arrest, seek legal advice, and examine and read the Codes of Practice.

Limits to detention

Nobody should be detained for longer than 24 hours without charge. A police officer with the rank of superintendent (or above) can authorize detention for a further 12 hours. Magistrates can authorize further detentions up to a maximum of 96 hours. Once charged, if a person is still in detention, they should be brought before the magistrates the next day (but not on Christmas Day, Good Friday, or any Sunday). At the time of writing, if a person is arrested as a suspected terrorist, different rules apply. A judge can authorize continued detention, in stages, for up to 28 days.

....

R (on the application of G) v Chief Constable of West Yorkshire [2008] 1WLR 550

The question was whether a custody officer was entitled to detain an arrested person whilst he sought guidance from the Crown Prosecution Service under **s 37A Police and Criminal Evidence Act 1984** on how to proceed with the charges.

The Court of Appeal held that **s 37(7) PACE** deals comprehensively with the alternatives available to a custody officer. These do not include a power to postpone the charging decision for the purpose of obtaining advice from the Crown Prosecution Service without admitting the suspect to bail. Such a power cannot be inferred by reference to guidance issued by the Director of Public Prosecutions. G's detention without charge was illegal.

....

Public order

Revision tip

At this stage in your revision you should link police powers and public order with the human rights principles discussed in chapter 14. There are also 'rule of law' implications to this topic which link up with material discussed in chapter 3. You should now take time to consider the material you revised in these chapters. Doing this will help you when answering essay questions in the examination.

The relevant statutes are the **Public Order Act 1986, Criminal Justice and Public Order Act 1994, Anti-social Behaviour Act 2003, Serious Organised Crime and Police Act 2005.**

Public Order Act 1986 as amended

Section 11 requires at least six clear days' written notice to be given to the police before most public processions, including details of the intended time and route, and giving the name and address of at least one person proposing to organize it. **Sections 12 to 14** give police power to impose conditions on processions 'to prevent serious public disorder, serious criminal damage or serious disruption to the life of the community'; ban public processions for up to three months by applying to local authority for a banning order which needs subsequent confirmation from the Home Secretary; impose conditions on assemblies 'to prevent serious public disorder, serious criminal damage or serious disruption to the life of the community'. The conditions are limited to the specifying of the number of people who may take part, the location of the assembly, and its maximum duration.

Criminal Justice and Public Order Act 1994

Sections 34–39 substantially changed the right to silence of an accused person, allowing for inferences to be drawn from their silence. **Sections 54–59** gave the police greater rights to take and retain intimate body samples. **Section 60** increased police powers of unsupervised 'stop and search'. **Section 70** prohibited trespassory assemblies.

Anti-social Behaviour Act 2003

Section 57 amends the definition of public assembly in **s 16 Public Order Act 1986** from '20 or more persons' to '2 or more persons'. **Section 58** amends **s 63 Criminal Justice and Public Order Act 1994** to extend it to cover raves where 20 or more persons are present. **Section 59** amends **ss 68 and 69 Criminal Justice and Public Order Act 1994**. Aggravated trespass covers trespass in buildings, as well as in the open air. **Section 60** inserts a new **s 62A** into the **Criminal Justice and Public Order Act 1994**. A senior police officer may direct a person to leave land and remove any vehicle or other property with him.

Serious Organised Crime and Police Act 2005

Apart from changing the rules governing arrest this Act created an exclusion zone of one kilometre from any point in Parliament Square within which the right to demonstrate is restricted. Trafalgar Square is not included. Demonstrators must apply to the Metropolitan Police Commissioner six days in advance, or if this is not reasonably practicable then no less than 24 hours in advance.

Austin v Commissioner of Police of the Metropolis [2007] EWCA 989

The Court of Appeal had to decide whether the police had been justified in depriving the claimants of their liberty, by cordoning them within an area for seven hours along with over 1000 protestors, on the ground that it was necessary to prevent a breach of the peace.

In extreme and exceptional circumstances it is lawful for the police to contain demonstrators and members of the public caught up in that demonstration, even though they themselves did not appear to be about to commit a breach of the peace, where it is necessary to prevent an imminent breach of the peace by others, and no other means would achieve that.

✅ Looking for extra marks?

Police powers and public order are highly controversial subjects which have given rise to a great deal academic argument. Some of these arguments are contained in articles referred to in the key debates section at the end of this guide. As essay questions, in particular, require you to demonstrate evidence of wider reading, you should read these articles, as well as those recommended in your course materials, and your recommended standard textbook.

Terrorism

Revision tip

This topic not only links up with human rights and the rule of law, as do police powers and public order but also with separation of powers considered in chapter 4. You should now reconsider the issues discussed in chapter 3. This will help you to answer any essay question which focuses on the relationship between the executive and the judiciary or the nature and extent of judicial independence.

According to **s 1 Terrorism Act 2000** as amended by the **Terrorism Act 2006**, terrorism means the use or threat of action involving serious violence against a person; or serious damage to property; or danger to life; or a serious risk to the health and safety of the public; or interference with an electronic system.

The use or threat of action must be designed to influence the government or an international governmental organization or to intimidate the public or a section of the public. The use or threat of action must be made for the purpose of advancing a political, religious, or ideological cause.

The **Terrorism Act 2000** made it illegal for certain terrorist groups to operate in the UK. The groups listed are called proscribed organizations and include international terrorist groups. The police were given greater powers to help prevent and investigate terrorism, including wider stop and search powers; and the power to detain suspects after arrest for up to 28 days (periods of more than two days must be approved by a magistrate). This period was extended to 28 days under the **Terrorism Act 2006**. A number of new offences were introduced allowing the police to arrest people suspected of inciting terrorist acts; seeking or providing training for terrorist purposes at home or overseas and providing instruction or training in the use of firearms, explosives, or chemical, biological, or nuclear weapons.

The **Anti-terrorism, Crime and Security Act 2001** aimed to cut off terrorist funding; ensure that government departments and agencies can collect and share information required for countering the terrorist threat; streamline relevant immigration procedures; ensure the security of the nuclear and aviation industries; improve security of dangerous substances that may be targeted/used by terrorists; extend police powers available to relevant forces; ensure that we can meet our European obligations in the area of police and judicial cooperation and our international obligations to counter bribery and corruption.

Revision tip

The measures enacted by the 2001 Act were considered by the House of Lords in *A v Secretary of State for the Home Department* (2005).

The **Prevention of Terrorism Act 2005** introduced **control orders**, which impose conditions on where a person can go and what they can do. These must be signed by the Home Secretary and confirmed by a judge within seven days. A control order may impose conditions banning possession or use of specified articles or substances; prohibiting the use of certain services, such as internet or phones; restricting work or business; restricting association or communication with certain individuals, or other people generally; restricting the person's place of residence or who is allowed into the premises; requiring the person to be at specified places or in a particular area at certain times or days; and restricting movements within the UK or international travel.

A control order may also contain a specific 24-hour ban on movements and requirements to surrender a passport; give access to specified people to his home; allow officials to search his home; let officials remove items from premises for tests; be monitored by electronic tagging or other means; provide information to an official on demand; and report at a specified time and place.

Secretary of State for the Home Department v JJ [2007] UKHL 45

Secretary of State for the Home Department v MB [2007] UKHL 46

Secretary of State for the Home Department v E [2007] UKHL 47

In all three cases, the House of Lords had to consider whether the obligations placed upon the appellants breached their rights under **Article 5 of the European Convention on Human Rights 1950**; compliance with the Secretary of State's duty under **s 8(2) HRA 1998** was a condition precedent to the making of an order; and, a control order constituted a criminal charge for the purposes of **Article 6** of the Convention; and procedures which allowed reliance on undisclosed material breached **Article 6**. The House of Lords determined, in these cases, that control orders must be subject to 'civil fair trial procedure', which has been breached in some cases by the 'special advocate procedure'. This procedure allows the Government to release sensitive information to terror suspects' security-screened lawyers, on the condition that this information is not passed on to the suspect. Moreover, the Law Lords ruled that control orders do not constitute a criminal penalty and hence do not engage the much stricter requirements of 'criminal fair trial procedure'. The cases were referred back to the High Court.

. . . .

The **Terrorism Act 2006** creates new offences including the following: acts preparatory to terrorism; incitement or encouragement to terrorism; dissemination of terrorist publications; terrorist training offences. The **Terrorism Act 2006** also makes amendments to existing legislation, including introducing warrants to enable the police to search any property owned or controlled by a terrorist suspect; extending terrorism stop and search powers to cover bays and estuaries; extending police powers to detain suspects after arrest for up to 28 days (though periods of more than two days must be approved by a judicial authority); improved search powers at ports; increased flexibility of the proscription regime, including the power to proscribe groups that glorify terrorism.

The Counter Terrorism Act 2008

The **Counter Terrorism Act 2008** amends the law on terrorism in a number of ways. Its provisions affect the gathering and sharing of information for, among other things, counter terrorist purposes. This includes the disclosure sharing of information by and with the security services. It also makes provisions relating to the post charge questioning of terrorism suspects, the prosecution and sentencing of those charged with terrorism offences, the financial aspects of terrorism, sensitive information, and the creation of new powers and offences relating to terrorism.

✅ Looking for extra marks?

This is a topic which has generated a huge debate, specific aspects of which may be examined as essay questions. As with other aspects of this topic, you should follow up your reading of this chapter with accounts of this debate in your recommended standard textbook and other materials recommended in the guides provided as part of your guide.

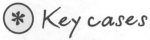 Key cases

Case	Facts	Principle
***A v Secretary of State for the Home Department* [2005] 2 AC 68**	The House of Lords had to decide whether s 23 of the Anti-terrorism, Crime and Security Act 2001 was compatible with Convention rights incorporated by the Human Rights Act 1998.	The House of Lords stated and applied the following principles: 1. personal liberty is among the most fundamental of rights; 2. although national security is a matter of political judgement for the executive and Parliament, a court is required, when Convention rights are in issue, to give effective protection by adopting an intensive review of whether such a right has been impugned; and 3. the courts are not precluded by any doctrine of deference from examining the proportionality of a measure taken to restrict such a right.
***Austin v Commissioner of Police of the Metropolis* [2007] EWCA 989**	The Court of Appeal had to decide whether the police had been justified in depriving the claimants of their liberty, by cordoning them within an area for seven hours along with over 1,000 protestors, on the ground that it was necessary to prevent a breach of the peace.	In extreme and exceptional circumstances it is lawful for the police to contain demonstrators and members of the public caught up in that demonstration even though they themselves did not appear to be about to commit a breach of the peace, where it is necessary to prevent an imminent breach of the peace by others, and no other means would achieve that.
***R (on the application of G) v Chief Constable of West Yorkshire* [2008] 1 WLR 550**	The question was whether a custody officer was entitled to detain an arrestee whilst he sought guidance from the Crown Prosecution Service under s 37A Police and Criminal Evidence Act 1984 on how to proceed with the charges.	Section 37(7) of the 1984 Act dealt comprehensively with the alternatives available to a custody officer who had determined that he had before him sufficient evidence to charge an arrested person; that those alternatives did not include a power to postpone the charging decision for the purpose of obtaining advice from the Crown Prosecution Service without admitting the suspect to bail; that such a power could not be inferred by reference to guidance issued by the Director of Public Prosecutions under s 37A, which was not referred to in s 37(7) which was required to be consistent with and limited by the alternatives found in that subsection.

Key debates

Topic	'Terrorism: Prevention of Terrorism Act 2005 ss. 2 and 3 – Non-derogating Control Order – Whether "Deprivation of Liberty" under Article 5 European Convention on Human Rights'
Author/Academic	Clive Walker
Viewpoint	Comments on three House of Lords' decisions on issues raised about non-derogating control orders made under **ss 2 and 3 Prevention of Terrorism Act 2005**.
Source	(2008) 6 Criminal Law Review 486–503.

Topic	'The Widening Gyre: Counter-terrorism, Human rights and the Rule of Law'
Author/Academic	Arthur Chaskalson
Viewpoint	Examines the parallels between some counter-terrorism measures introduced around the world in the wake of the US attacks of September 11, 2001 and the legal regime introduced in South Africa to support the policy of apartheid.
Source	(2008) 67(1) Cambridge Law Journal 69–91.

Topic	'Evidence and Procedure: Pre-charge Detention'
Author/Academic	Case comment
Viewpoint	Notes the Court of Appeal decision in **R (on the application of G) v Chief Constable of West Yorkshire (2008)**.
Source	(2008) 8 Criminal Law Week 1–3.

Topic	'Evidence and procedure: Stop and search'
Author/Academic	Case comment
Viewpoint	Reports of the Court of Appeal decision in **R v Bristol (Christopher) (2007)**.
Source	(2008) 3 Criminal Law Week 1–2.

Topic	'May Day, May Day: Policing Protest'
Author/Academic	ATH Smith
Viewpoint	Discusses the Court of Appeal decision in **Austin v Commissioner of Police of the Metropolis (2007)**.
Source	(2008) 67(1) Cambridge Law Journal 10–12.

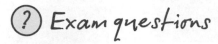

Essay question 1

Explain the nature and extent of police powers to detain suspects and indicate how these powers are limited.

Essay question 2

Critically assess the effectiveness of the Serious Organised Crime and Police Act 2005 as a means of controlling protest in Central London.

Scan here

Scan this QR code image with your mobile device to see outline answers to these questions or log onto www.oxfordtextbooks.co.uk/orc/concentrate

Exam essentials

Tips on linking the topics together

You need to acquire a thorough knowledge of the whole subject in order to achieve first class marks in the examination. Nothing less than a complete answer will do. This requires awareness of how topics are related to each other. In Public Law the topics link together in a number of ways.

Revision exercise: Note down areas of Public Law which you can draw links between and ways in which they are related.

Some examples of topics which are linked appear at the end of this guide.

Additionally, you should, by now, have acquired a set of past examination papers as part of your course materials. Read through them and note how the topics are combined.

Pointers for key topics/questions often tested

The key topics, which are unavoidably tested each year in Public Law examinations, will have been thoroughly covered by your subject lecturers and tutors in lectures and seminars. Review your Study Guide/Learning Materials together with your lecture and seminar notes. Record how much time was spent on each topic and the amount of detail and advice on further reading that was given to you by your lecturers and tutors. Read and analyse the past examination papers provided by your college or university. This analysis should cover between three to five years depending on what is available to you. Read all the questions and identify the topics tested in each question. List the topics in order from the most tested to the least tested topic.

Material to read and reference

At this point you should read and reference the key principles by reviewing your lecture notes, the relevant sections in your text book, and this revision guide.

Common mistakes to avoid

Before the examination

Don't :

- leave revision to the last minute;
- restrict your revision topics to the number of questions you are required to answer in the examination in the hope that your questions come up; or
- adopt an unstructured and un-timetabled approach to revision.

Above all don't panic!

During the examination

The most common mistakes students make during the examination could be avoided if they did the following:

- read through the whole of the examination paper during reading time and write out an outline answer giving essential details including cases and statutes to each question;
- answer every question in the examination paper that they are expected to answer; and
- organize their time effectively by dividing up their time as equally as may be between all the questions.

Ideas for revision activities

Find out about your exam

Find out about the examination. Obtain past examination papers and read them thoroughly. How long is the examination? Do you have reading time? How many questions do you have to answer? How many of the questions are problem based or essay type?

Work out what you need to know

Review your notes and materials looking for gaps in your knowledge of key topics which are often tested. Make a list of things you need to know to top up your knowledge. Locate, read, and extract the information you need to fill the gaps.

Make a revision timetable

Set aside time each day for your revision and stick to it. It is better to do an hour each day of the week than seven hours on a Friday!

Have a programme of activities

Your lecturers and tutors may have organized a programme of revision activities as part of your course. If so you should follow their guidance and participate fully in the programme. In addition, the following may help:

- active reading in which you choose a past examination question on the topic you are revising and as you read use the material you are reading to answer the question.
- plan and answer past exam questions under timed conditions. Review your answers and look for ways to improve them;
- review your assignments; and
- review, reorganize, and refine your notes.

Commonly linked topics in Public Law

The following list is not exhaustive.

- constitutional conventions link up with the monarchy and royal prerogative, the executive, the nature and functions of Parliament, and the legislative process;

- rule of law links up with separation of powers, tribunals, judicial review, and human rights;

- separation of powers may be linked to human rights, judicial review, tribunals, and the rule of law;

- sovereignty of Parliament may be linked to separation of powers, the monarchy as part of the legislative process, constitutional conventions, and the royal prerogative in relation to Parliament and the legislative process and human rights; and

- European Union law may be linked up with sovereignty of parliament;

- tribunals link up with rule of law, separation of powers, and judicial review.

Outline answers

Chapter 2

Problem answer

Parties and causes of action

The Prime Minister = Claimant

The Leader of the Opposition = Defendant

Cause of Action: Application for a Mandatory Injunction

The Prime Minister would first have to establish the relevant constitutional conventions

Reference re Amendment to the Constitution of Canada (1982):

- are there precedents?
- do the actors consider themselves bound?
- is there a good reason for the rule?

Define relevant conventions:

- Government must have the confidence of the House of Commons;
- if the Government loses the confidence of the House of Commons the Prime Minister should offer the Queen his resignation and ask for dissolution of Parliament and a General Election;
- the Queen is bound to accept the Government's resignation; and
- in the event of a General Election the Queen must ask the leader of the party with a majority in the House of Commons to form a government.

Apply *Attorney General v Jonathan Cape Ltd* (1975) grounds: it is against the public interest for the Government to remain in office without the confidence of the House of Commons; that there is no other facet of the public interest in conflict with and more compelling than that relied upon; and that the Prime Minister's course of action is unconstitutional.

The Prime Minister's counter arguments

The court has no jurisdiction to grant the injunction because constitutional conventions are not enforceable in the courts – *Madzimbamuto v Larder Burke* (1969).

That because he has really 'won' the election by polling more votes than the Opposition his continuance in office will not prejudice the constitutional convention that the Government must have the confidence of the House of Commons; and that his continuance in office is not contrary to the public interest.

This is based on *Attorney General v Jonathan Cape Ltd* (1975).

Conclusion – the court would probably decline jurisdiction.

The constitutional position of the Queen

You should break this stage down into two parts.

Part one: the Queen's legal powers

The Queen is the only person authorized to:

- dissolve (prorogue) and call Parliaments;
- appoint ministers; and
- appoint a prime minister and ask him or her to form a government.

The source of these powers is common law under the Royal Prerogative.

Part two: constitutional conventions

Whether the Queen is obliged to accept the Prime Minister's resignation; and whom she may ask to form the next government.

The relevant conventions are:

- the Queen acts on the advice of ministers; and
- Her Majesty's Government must have the confidence of the House of Commons.

You should explain the consequences:

- she may wait to see if the Prime Minister can form a coalition government;
- if not she is obliged to accept the Prime Minister's resignation; and
- ask the leader of the party with a majority in the House of Commons to form a government.

Outline answers
✱✱✱✱✱✱✱✱✱✱✱✱

Chapter 5
∙∙∙

Problem answer

The answer to this question breaks down into the following sections:

Introduction

In your introduction, you should identify the issues raised by the question and define any concepts or principles which form the basis of the question. In particular you should indicate that:

• the Royal Prerogative forms the basis of the monarch's powers in both parts of the question and emphasize that it is essentially the residue of arbitrary and discretionary power exercised by the Crown;

• the Crown, in this context, means the personal powers of the monarch acting as head of state;

• constitutional conventions play an important role in determining how the monarch's powers are to be exercised; and

• explain Dicey's definition of constitutional conventions in terms of political rules which are not enforceable in the courts.

Part one – the appointment of the Prime Minister

Identify the monarch's legal (Royal Prerogative) powers to:

• dissolve (prorogue) and call Parliaments;

• appoint ministers; and

• appoint a Prime Minister and ask him or her to form a government.

Identify and state the relevant constitutional conventions, namely:

• the Queen acts on the advice of ministers; and

• Her Majesty's Government must have the confidence of the House of Commons.

It is important to point out at this stage that the monarch is normally obliged to appoint the leader of the party with a majority of seats in the House of Commons.

Once you have discussed the elements, nature, and scope of the relevant constitutional conventions you should go on to look at how this would influence the monarch's conduct in the present scenario. You can refer to the example of the outcome of the 1974 General Elections when there was no clear Labour majority in the House of Commons.

One possible outcome is that Queen may wait to see if Mr Cameron can form a coalition government; if not she is obliged to accept Mr Cameron's resignation; and ask the leader of the party with a majority in the House of Commons to form a government.

Royal Assent

In this part of your answer you should explain that:

• it is a legal requirement for a bill to receive the Royal Assent before it can become an Act of Parliament;

• the basis of the monarch's power is the Royal Prerogative;

• the legal power to grant the Royal Assent carries with it the right to refuse the Royal Assent;

• there is an important constitutional convention to the effect that the royal assent will be granted as a matter of course.

You should illustrate your answer with examples like the Scottish Militia Bill in the reign of Queen Anne and the Government of Ireland Bill in the reign of George V. You should also refer to the arguments on this issue presented in this chapter.

It is unlikely that any monarch would refuse the Royal Assent.

Chapter 6
∙∙∙

Problem answer

Introduction

In this part of your answer it is important to emphasise that the Home Secretary's position is governed by constitutional conventions which cannot be enforced in the courts. Distinguish between law and convention (Dicey).

Collective Cabinet responsibility

You should begin by defining collective Cabinet responsibility in the way that Lord Widgery CJ did in *Attorney General v Jonathan Cape (1975)*.

You should stress that that the obligation is a political rather than a legal one.

The political and legal accountability of the Home Secretary

According to the **Crichel Down Principle** based on the Crichel Down Affair (1954) accountability arises when a civil servant:

- has carried out the minister's explicit order;
- acts in accordance with policy laid down by the minister; or
- makes a mistake or causes a delay.

As to whether the Home Secretary is politically bound to resign, you should consider:

- Matrix Churchill
- The Scott Report Findings
- The Report of the Public Service Committee

The legal accountability of the Home Secretary

The relevant principle is that ministers have legal responsibility for whatever happens in their departments. It is the minister who is sued, not the civil servant. The courts accept and recognize the convention that a civil servant often acts in the name of ministers. The relevant case law is:

- *Carltona v Commissioners of Works* (1943)
- *R v Skinner* (1968)
- *R v Secretary of State for the Home Department, ex p Oladehinde* (1991)
- *M v Home Office* (1993)

Chapter 8
....

Problem answer

Introduction

In this part of your answer you should identify: the parties, the causes of action, and the issues.

The jurisdictional issue

The relevant case law is:

- *Stockdale v Hansard* (1839)
- *Edinburgh & Dalkeith Railway v Wauchope* (1842)

- *Lee v Bude & Torrington Junction Railway* (1871)
- *Pickin v British Rail Board* (1974)

The effect of sections 2 and 3 of the 2005 Act

In this part of your answer you should: define express and implied repeal; define 'entrenchment'; apply the rule that Parliament cannot bind its successors.

Elizabeth could rely on:

- *Vauxhall Estates Ltd v Liverpool Corporation* (1932)
- *Ellen Street Estates v Minister of Health* (1934)

The doctor could rely on:

- *R v Military Governor of NDU Internment Camp* (1924)
- *AG of New South Wales v Trethowan* (1932)
- *Harris v Minister of the Interior* (1952)

Conclusion: entrenchment clauses are not effective against express or implied repeal.

Prospective formula

Here, you should define prospective formula and explain its effect on express and implied repeal. If the 2006 Act expressly repeals the 2005 Act, the 2006 Act prevails.

Chapter 10
....

Problem answer

Introduction

In this part of your answer you should identify: the parties, the causes of action, the issues.

The jurisdictional issue

All a court can do is interpret and apply an Act of Parliament once it has received the separate but simultaneous assents of the House of Commons and House of Lords plus the Royal Assent. The relevant case law is:

- *Stockdale v Hansard* (1839)
- *Edinburgh & Dalkeith Railway v Wauchope* (1842)
- *Lee v Bude & Torrington Junction Railway* (1871)
- *Pickin v British Rail Board* (1974)

Outline answers
✶✶✶✶✶✶✶✶✶✶✶✶

You should consider whether this applies where EU Law is concerned.

Express and implied repeal

The underlying question is whether **s 2 European Communities Act 1972** is protected from amendment or repeal. In this part of your answer you should define express and implied repeal. The relevant case law is:

- *Vauxhall Estates Ltd v Liverpool Corporation* (1932)
- *Ellen Street Estates v Minister of Health* (1934)

Once you have explained these rules, you must consider whether a clause in an Act of Parliament can effectively protect a statute from amendment or repeal.

Prospective formula

You should begin this section of your answer by looking at **s 2(4) European Communities Act 1972**. Then you should consider:

- **Section 2 European Communities Act 1972**
- *R v Secretary of State for Transport, ex p Factortame* (1989)
- *Stoke-on-Trent City Council v B & Q plc* (1991)
- *Equal Opportunities Commission v Secretary of State for Employment* (1994)

Finally you should discuss *Thoburn v Sunderland City Council* and decide whether the Court would, in this case, disapply the provisions of the 2009 Act. You should also indicate that, following *Factortame No 1*, **s 2 European Communities Act 1972** is not subject to the doctrine of implied repeal.

Chapter 11
· ·

Problem answer

Introduction – parties and causes of action

Claimant = Antonio

Defendant = The Food Standards Authority

Interested Party = Society of Ice Cream Manufacturers

Cause of Action = for judicial review. He will ask a judge to review the lawfulness of the decision of the Food Standards Authority.

Is the Food Standards Authority amenable to judicial review?

First consider *Datafin* criteria, bearing in mind that all the criteria have to be considered. *R v Panel on Take-overs and Mergers, ex p Datafin* (1987).

Consider whether: the functions of the Food Standards Authority are governmental; it is an integral part of a Government-supported scheme of regulation; and, would the Government introduce legislation through Parliament to set up a regulatory body if the Food Standards Authority did not exist. Key case:

- *R v Disciplinary Committee of the Jockey Club, ex p Aga Khan* (1993).

Is the decision of the Food Standards Authority a public law matter?

Consider whether the context of the decision is the exercise of a public function and whether the claimant would be accused of abuse of process if he brought a claim using private law procedure. Key cases:

- *O'Reilly v Mackman* (1982)
- *Clark v University of Lincolnshire and Humberside* (2000).

Does the Society of Ice Cream Manufacturers have the right to bring a claim for judicial review?

You should consider whether, in your opinion, the organization has sufficient interest taking into account all the relevant criteria set out in the cases above. Key cases:

- *IRC v National Federation of the Self-Employed and Small Businesses* (1981)
- *R v Inspectorate of Pollution, ex p Greenpeace* (1994)
- *R v Secretary for State for Foreign Affairs, ex p World Development Movement* (1995).

Remedies and procedure

You should choose a remedy or combination of remedies and explain its effect. Then you should outline the initial procedural steps.

Chapter 12

Problem answer

Parties and causes of action

Claimant = Justin

Defendants = The Commission and the Secretary of State

Cause of Action = Judicial Review. The defendants are public authorities and the decisions being challenged are public law matters. (*O'Reilly v Mackman* (1983))

Basic procedural steps

Pre-action Protocol:

• Alternative dispute resolution

• Letter before claim

• Letter in response

Commencement of proceedings under s 1 Part 54 **Civil Procedure Rules:**

• application for permission

• to Administrative Court

• within three months of the decision

• using appropriate claim form; and

• supporting documents.

Grounds for judicial review

Has the defendant acted *ultra vires*. Define *ultra vires*. Relevant case law includes:

• *AG v Fulham Corporation* (1921)

• *Bromley LBC v GLC* (1983)

In this question, the following grounds, with reference to relevant cases, are to be considered:

Improper purpose

The relevant case law to which you should refer includes:

• *Congreve v Home Office* (1976)

• *R v Lewisham LBC, ex p Shell* (1988)

• *Wheeler v Leicester City Council* (1985)

Relevant considerations

• *R v Secretary of State for the Home Department, ex p Venables and Thompson* (1998)

Lack of evidence

• *Coleen Properties v Minister of Housing and Local Government* (1971)

Fettering discretion by policy

• *British Oxygen Co Ltd v Minster of Technology* (1971)

Remedies

Choose the remedy you think is most appropriate. In this case it would be a quashing order to nullify the decision.

Glossary

Abuse of process In the context of judicial review, this means the unreasonable use of civil procedure for the purpose of gaining unfair advantage over an opponent in a legal dispute.

Ad hoc committees '*Ad hoc*' means 'for this purpose'. An *ad hoc* committee is set up by Parliament for a specific reason and ceases to exist when its task is finished.

Collective Cabinet responsibility Any policy decision reached by the Cabinet has to be supported thereafter by all members of the Cabinet whether they approve of it or not, unless they feel compelled to resign.

Common law The common law is made up of judge-made rules applied in decided cases which apply throughout England and Wales.

Constitutional practices or conventions Informal political rules adopted by those who participate in the process of government, which are considered binding to a varying extent but which are not enforceable in the courts.

Control order These impose conditions on where a person can go and what they can do.

Convention right In the **Human Rights Act 1998**, 'Convention right' means:

1. The rights contained in **Articles 2 to 12 and 14 European Convention on Human Rights and Fundamental Freedoms**;

2. **Articles 1 to 3 of the First Protocol**; and

3. **Articles 1 and 2 of the Sixth Protocol.**

Crown proceedings In English law, Crown proceedings are legal proceedings which involve the executive governed by the **Crown Proceedings Act 1947**.

Delegated legislation Regulations and other laws made by Government ministers empowered to do so by statute. The empowering statute may require such regulations to be scrutinized and approved by Parliament before they come into effect.

Directive A directive is a legislative act of the European Union which requires Member States to achieve a particular result without dictating the means of achieving that result. It can be distinguished from European Union regulations which are self-executing and do not require any implementing measures. Directives can be adopted by means of a variety of legislative procedures depending on the subject matter.

His/Her Majesty's Principal Secretaries of State Senior ministers who lead most, but not all central government departments. They are members of the Privy Council and the Cabinet.

Illegality In Lord Diplock's words, this ground means that the decision-maker must understand correctly the law that regulates his decision-making power and must give effect to it.

Injunction This is a discretionary court order which can be used to stop something being done or require something to be discontinued. It can also be used to order something to be done.

Judicial review According to the Pre-Action Protocol on Judicial Review: judicial review allows people with a sufficient interest in a decision or action of a public body to ask a judge to review the lawfulness of:

- an enactment; or
- a decision, action or failure to act in relation to the exercise of a public function.

Jurisdictional error At common law, jurisdictional error developed as a ground of review which was available where a tribunal or inferior court (as opposed to an administrator such as a minister or public servant) purported to exercise jurisdiction in excess of that which had been conferred upon it, or failed to exercise jurisdiction which it properly had.

Justiciability This means that a matter is capable of being decided by a court.

Glossary
****

Ministers of the Crown A minister of the Crown is the formal constitutional term used to describe a member of His/Her Majesty's Government. Secretaries of State are ministers of the Crown. The term indicates that the person appointed serves in theory at His/Her Majesty's Pleasure, and advises the monarch. In practice, all ministers of the Crown are members of and are accountable to Parliament.

Non-jurisdictional error Under the traditional doctrine, non-jurisdictional (ie non-judicially reviewable unless on the face of the record) errors, are errors of law made by a tribunal or inferior court in the course of exercising jurisdiction which it properly has.

Ouster clause Any provision of an Act of Parliament which purports to limit or exclude the supervisory jurisdiction of the High Court.

Preliminary ruling To ensure the effective and uniform application of Community legislation and to prevent divergent interpretations, national courts may, and sometimes must, turn to the Court of Justice and ask that it clarify a point concerning the interpretation of Community law, in order, for example, to ascertain whether their national legislation complies with that law.

Private Members' Bills Private Members' Bills are Public Bills introduced by MPs and Lords who are not government ministers. As with other Public Bills their purpose is to change the law as it applies to the general population.

Procedural impropriety A decision suffers from procedural impropriety if, in the process of its making a decision, the procedures prescribed by statute have not been followed or if the 'rules of natural justice' have not been adhered to.

Proportionality Proportionality is a requirement that a decision is proportionate to the aim that it seeks to achieve.

Public Accounts Committee The Committee of Public Accounts is appointed by the House of Commons to examine the accounts showing the appropriation of the sums granted by Parliament to meet the public expenditure, and of such other accounts laid before Parliament as the Committee may think fit.

Public authority According to s 6(3) **Human Rights Act 1998** 'public authority' includes:

(a) a court or tribunal, and

(b) any person certain of whose functions are functions of a public nature,

but does not include either House of Parliament or a person exercising functions in connection with proceedings in Parliament.

Public body Any organization whose functions are of a governmental nature whose powers are not wholly based on agreement.

Public interest This is a wide subjective principle usually referring to the safety and welfare of the state.

Public interest immunity This is a principle of English common law under which the English courts can grant a court order allowing one litigant to refrain from disclosing evidence to the other litigants where disclosure would be damaging to the public interest. This is an exception to the usual rule that all parties in litigation must disclose any evidence that is relevant to the proceedings. In making a PII order, the court has to balance the public interest in the administration of justice (which demands that relevant material is available to the parties to litigation) and the public interest in maintaining the confidentiality of certain documents whose disclosure would be damaging.

Regulation A regulation is a legislative act of the European Union which becomes immediately enforceable as law in all Member States simultaneously. Regulations can be distinguished from directives which, at least in principle, need to be transposed into national law.

Republic A country which has an executive or non-executive president as head of state.

Royal Assent The monarch's acceptance of a parliamentary bill which has either received the necessary assents of the House of Lords and the House of Commons or has received the assent of the House of Commons under the **Parliament Acts 1911 and 1949**.

Royal Commissions A Royal Commission is a major government public inquiry into an issue.

Royal Prerogative The judicially accepted definition of Royal Prerogative is that it represents the residue of arbitrary and discretionary power possessed by the Crown.

Rule of law The rule of law implies the equal subordination of governmental bodies to the substantive and procedural requirements of the law so as to prevent them exercising purely arbitrary and discretionary power. It also embodies the idea that everyone is equally subject to the law and that the rights of citizens are protected by the legal system.

Separation of powers The separation of powers is capable of meaning that:

- the same persons should not form part of more than one of the three organs of government;
- one organ of government should not control or interfere with the work of another; and
- one organ of government should not exercise the functions of another.

Standing Committees These are established by an official and binding vote providing for their scope and powers. 'Standing', in this context means that they are permanent. Standing committees meet on a regular or irregular basis dependent upon their enabling act, and retain any power or oversight claims originally given them until subsequent official actions of the committee of the whole (changes to law or by-laws) disbands the committee or changes their duties and powers.

Supremacy of law In this context it means that governmental power is based on law rather than arbitrary force exercisable with absolute discretion.

Ultra vires This is a Latin phrase that literally means 'beyond the powers'.

Unreasonableness Under Lord Diplock's classification, a decision is irrational if it is so outrageous in its defiance of logic or of accepted moral standards that no sensible person who had applied his mind to the question could have arrived at it.

Victim Under **s 7(7) Human Rights Act 1998** a person is a victim of an unlawful act only if he would be a victim for the purposes of **Article 34** of the Convention if proceedings were brought in the European Court of Human Rights in respect of that act.

Whip system The aim of the whip system is to maintain party discipline within Parliament. Whips are MPs or Peers appointed by each party to maintain party discipline. In a sense they are personnel managers who convey information between party leaders and back bench members. Part of their role, however, is to encourage members of their party to vote in the way that their party would like.

Index

Index

Index

Index

****